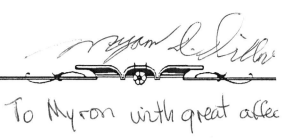

To Myron with great affec

HOME BY THE FOURTH OF JULY

the story of William Francis Kimmell
Life in the 8th Regiment, Ohio Volunteer Infantry

Eleanor

Excerpts from his letters and diary

Additions from William Franklin Sawyer's
"A Military History of the 8th Regiment, Ohio Volunteer Infantry"
Published 1881

Compiled by Eleanor Kimmell Roubique
Copyright 1995

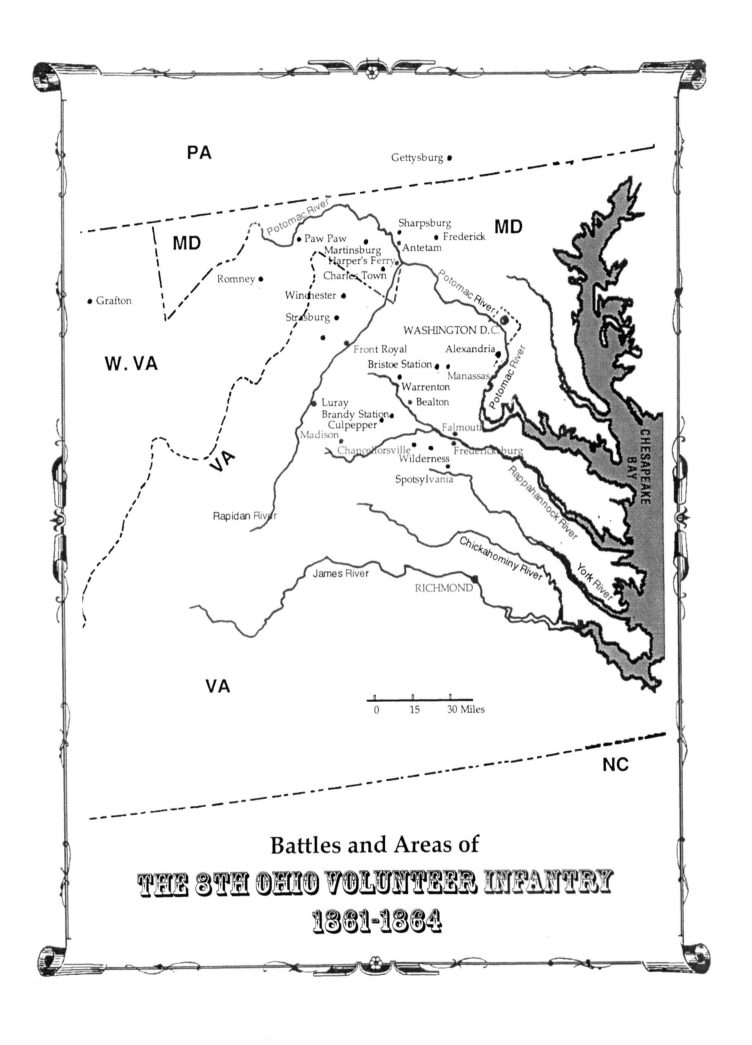

Battles and Areas of

THE 8TH OHIO VOLUNTEER INFANTRY
1861-1864

Wm T. Kimmell

DEDICATION

To my brother, Arnold C. Kimmell, whose encouragement and interest in my search for grandfather's story gave me the push to research; to my husband, Charles J. Roubique, whose unflagging help in search, motor home trips, library time, copying, reading of maps and constant love, without which I would flounder; to my late parents, Anthony Crispell Kimmell and Luella B. Prickett whose interest in things gone by were given to me at an early age; my Kimmell cousins whose interest in W. F. and Leah was as eager as mine; to my daughters and grand-children, to whom I hope these words will be important, and finally, a huge thank you to Jeff Bell for his editing, composing and making this story readable.

Eleanor
1995

INTRODUCTION

When I was a little girl and had just learned to read, I often entertained myself by reading Grandfather Kimmell's letters from the Civil War. I always fantasized about what he was like and how tall he was, whether or not Leah Crispell would have liked me.Did she have brown eyes and did she have curly red-brown hair like mine? I even practiced my artithmetic subtracting and adding ages to see how old he would be when I was born and could he possibly be alive when I was 6?

Both of my grandparents died when my father, Anthony Crispell Kimmell, was a child. Leah passed away six weeks after my father was born in Pitkin, Colorado in 1887, and William F., died in 1892 from pneumonia related causes at Chattanooga, Tennessee. He was the assistant superintendent of the National Military Cemetery located there.

My father was raised by Leah's sister, Catharine Crispell Foote and her husband, Calvin, in Albion, Indiana.

How fortunate that these wonderful bits of my grandparents were treasured by my family and that I inherited them.

My husband, Charles Roubique, was so enamored of these fragile pieces that he copied them on the Xerox machine so that we would not lose them to neglect and age. I have shared them with my cousins and anyone who wanted to read or listen. Several years ago, my cousin, Bertha Kimmel Myers, gave me copies of the diary that W. F. had kept during the first portion of his military service and which he sent to his sister, Eliza Haas of Albion, Indiana.

This was a most welcome addition to my "history". While on a genealogical research expedition to the Denver Public Library I discovered the out of print book written by Colonel Franklin Sawyer, the regimental commander of the 8th Ohio. I made a copy of this for my own use and read this story many times, but did not have the urge to do anything about combining these two bits of history into one readable story for my family until Catharine Louisa Moore, of Richmond, Virginia told me that she had been assigned to write something about the civil war. What greater opportunity for me to share my story with a young person who was literally on the site of W. F. Kimmell's young soldier life than this comment from her. It was then that I began to compile the two men's stories into one. It has been a sad journey as well as one of pleasure. Sad because of the unnecessary loss to both sides of the battle, and pleasurable because I was at last able to understand the loneliness, frustration, devastation and despair that my grandfather had gone through for three years and four months.

The letters are written from a period January 1861 to June 7, 1864. They are an interesting comment on the life of a soldier and reflect the lonlieness and longing for home that is typical of a boy away from his family. The diary tells in more detail the events that shaped the course of the war. W. F.'s letters touch briefly on the battles he was in and the routine and boredom of camp life. They primarily dealt with his friendship with Leah, the gossip written by other residents of Albion, and what he wants to do when he gets home. (Most often by the 4th of July.) W. F.'s spelling and punctuation show his lack of formal education and his lack of maturity. These short comings change as he grew to manhood during his enlistment time. (W. F. later began a newspaper in Albion, with his brother A. J., called the "Albion Advertiser." He also edited a paper in Osceola, Nebraska, a town he helped plat in 1870.)

Sawyer's book A Military History of the 8th Regiment Ohio Volunteer Infantry reflects more on the military part of the battles. Col. Franklin Sawyer was commissioned to write his memoirs by a committee of regiment survivors in 1879 at a reunion of the 8th Ohio in Norwalk, Ohio,

Sawyer had previously begun to write about the events but it was not until the committee was formed to help Sawyer write the book that he completed the task. The memoirs were published in 1881. Col. Sawyer's account begins at the forming of the Regiment in Bucyrus.

The 8th Ohio was involved in many of the major battles of the Civil War fought in Virginia, Maryland, and Pennsylvania. From W. F.'s war records secured from the National Archives, I learned that he that he had been wounded twice. and was five feet 6 inches tall with brown hair and brown eyes. His height was a surprise to the family because we had all pictured him as being a large man since his sons were 6 feet tall and over. Perhaps it was the many places and events that WF was involved in his very short life that made us feel his imposing stature. Military records also indicated that W. F.'s application for invalid pension was based on his debilitating asthma which he acquired from "standing in water filled trenches."

William was born in Canton, Ohio in 1842, the son of Adam and Elizabeth Bowers Kimmell. He was the youngest in the family. His mother died in 1849 when William was 7 years old. Adam Kimmell moved to Noble County, Indiana in 1854 with William. Older children of Adam also were living in Indiana when Adam made his move from Canton. They were Joseph, Adam J. (known as A. J.),Manias H., Eliza Kimmell Haas and Lucinda Kimmell Casper.

William spent his youth in this community. He had learned the trade of tinner and had lived for a time in Ft. Wayne, Indiana after attending school in Albion. According to the diary he wrote of his wartime experiences he had been moving about and just happened to be in Bucyrus, Ohio when the call for volunteers came from the Governor of Ohio.

Leah, the recipient of many of the letters W. F. wrote during his army service lived on her family's farm which was near Albion, Indiana and the Crispell sisters and the Kimmell boy enjoyed many youthful activities in each other's company.

W. F. sent his diary to his sister, Eliza Haas, explaining that he thought she would enjoy reading of his experiences much more if written in this form.

The letters will be identified by Italics, the diary will be noted and Colonel Sawyer's comments will be in quotations. Maps showing locations of the 8th Ohio will be included.

Eleanor Kimmell Roubique

Arvada, Colorado 1995

HOME BY THE FOURTH OF JULY

The War Proclamation calling for 75,000 volunteers had just been issued by President Abraham Lincoln on April 14, 1861 and all over the country, on both sides, much political and patriotic fervor was evidenced. In Bucyrus, Ohio the call was out for volunteers to serve for a three month period in the armed services. A great rally had been held on the 17th day of April and according to the diary written by William Francis Kimmell, an eager 19 year old man from Albion, Indiana, he was the second person in line at the recruiting station to put his name on the list for service. The group was called "The Bucyrus Light Infantry."

The group of enrollees from Bucyrus were formed into Company C of the 8th Regiment Ohio Volunteer Infantry. They were detailed to Camp Taylor at Cleveland, Ohio to be mustered into service. The commanding officer was Franklin Sawyer, Lt. Col and later breveted Brigadier General.

Franklin Sawyer said, "The question was not, 'Who will go?' but 'Who and how many of us will the government accept?'

"For Northern Ohio, Camp Taylor at Cleveland, was the place of rendezvous. Governor Dennison's order was dated the 16th day of April, 1861, and in a few days several thousand men, partially organized had assembled at Camp Taylor, anxious to be mustered into the service. Out of this, the 8th Ohio Volunteer Infantry was formed."

The first letter written to Leah from W. F. Kimmell was datelined Camp Dennison, June 30, 1861.

Dear Friends Leah and Kate,

You will be surprised to get a letter from me way in this part of the world, but it is nothing strange. I will say nothing of how I got here, supposing you know as well as I can tell you.

At any rate, I am here a United States soldier enlisted for three years and hoping to do something for my country before I come home again.

I was very sorry that I could not come to see you when I was at home but time would not permit it. But I shall see you next time I get home and expect to see you both married and with families.

I was overhauling some of my personal property this morning and came across your likenesses and it put me in mind of a forgotten promise which I shall fulfill that is in sending you my likeness.

It is taken in full uniform and will give you some idea of my looks as a soldier. Your likenesses are the only thing that I have that reminds me of home and I prize them very highly. I have often wondered what was the reason that our correspondence was broken off. I am shure that I am not to blame for it. I wrote you two or three letters and received no answer and thought you did not get them or that they were not acceptable, but could not make up my mind that such was the case. So I shall write this to see what is the matter.

If you have any beaus let me know who they are and what the prospects of marriage is for to tell the truth, I believe you are both old enough to marry. I am

tired writing and you must excuse my bad writing for I handle the musket more than I do the pen. Give my best respects to all and write soon. Direct to

Wm F. Kimmell
care of Capt Butterfield,
Co C 8th Regt.
Camp Dennison, Ohio
    P.S. Tell my folks that I have got my health perfectly and can eat my ration of pork and beans and more to. I shall write home next week.
WK

WF's diary referred to this stay at Camp Dennison in this manner. "We passed the time very plesently, our only trouble was we could not get enough to eat. What we did get was half cooked. Camp Dennison is on the Little Miami R. R. fifteen miles above Cincinnati. We expected to find Barracks for our accomodation. You can imagine our feelin's when we found ourselves landed in a big wheat field and the rain coming down. There was not a board or a shelter of any kind to go under we had nothing else to do but lay down in the mud and pass the night as best we could."

Col. Sawyer's comments from his book **A Military History of the 8th Regiment Ohio Volunteer Infantry** reveal that the men suffered much from sickness, especially from measles, which broke out in camp.

The diary describes the camp in this manner, "During the day we got boards and put up shanties. Our shanties were 11 x 21 feet—six of them to a company. We soon got to living very comfortable. Chickens got very scarce in the neighborhood."

Colonel Sawyer remarked that the Regiment had acquired a considerable proficiency in drill and after the three month enlistment period had passed, the Regiment was re-organized into the group which was to stay together for the entire period of enlistment. "On the 8th of July 1861, the Regiment received orders to move that day and with its tents, baggage, etc., was embarked toward Grafton, VA (now West Virginia).

"The men were noisy and jolly all night and had little sleep. When daylight came, the road side was literally lined with people who had congregated along the route to cheer us onward."

W. F."s diary entry, "We were at Fetterman, two miles from Grafton, the 11th here we rested over night after traveling about three hundred miles. That night we staked out in line of battle expecting an attact. No enemy within fifty miles.

Referring to the same incident, Col. Sawyer remarked that the enemy proved to be "an inquisitive cow who had approached one of the sentinels who fired, dispersing the cow and summarily arousing the troops. This fact having been ascertained by our commander, we fell back in good order to our bunks. "

On the morning of the 12th of July, the Regiment was ordered to set out for Uniontown, the only trouble they met was with some women who ran a mill and the chaplain. The chaplain asked the women to allow them to house some of the sick men in the mill out of the weather. The chaplain prevailed."

The WFK diary describes the outfit. "Each man carried his knap sack. Blanket, haversack with two days rations, canteen full of water. Gun cartridge box and belt, weighing in all near one hundred pounds. Pretty good load you will think. Well it proved so soon enough we had not gone far untill some of the weaker ones began todrop off. It soon began to rain. It rained very near the whole time of our march. We got to West Union late in the night wet tired and hungry."

Sawyer stated that the troops spent about 10 days marching and building a camp called Camp Pendleton because of the plantation located at this spot. The camp was in this area because it was on the principal road over the mountains, leading from Western Virginia to Romney and Winchester, and was regarded as an important thoroughfare.

Sawyer remarked, "The camp was in a most unhealthy location being down in a deep, damp gorge in the mountain; the men soon began to get sick, and in a few days, about three hundred were in hospital.

"The disease was a low type of fever. The men called it the disease of 'Camp Maggotty Hollow,' the name they had given the camp."

WF's diary said that the camp was called Camp Maggot because of the "immence swarms of maggots" that travelled up and down it every day. "Here we commenced building fortifications. Working on that together with the guard duty made it very hard on us. Often have I thought while here that if I was out of the army I would not be very apt to enlist again. The maggots finaly conquered and we had to leave there the 8th of August."

Sawyer detailed the departure of the troops on the 23rd of September 1861 on an expedition to capture Romney. "The troops were countermarched across the river, which was deep and rapid at this point, and had to be forded to the opposite bank, when a halt was made. There was a dense fog hanging over the river, which prevented further operations. The fog cleared away around noon and another attempt was made to enter Romney in this direction. The troops crossed and recrossed the river to a point near Mechanicsburg Gap. The troops found the rebel outposts and drove in upon them.

"We held the place for a couple of hours and, fearing the enemy was receiving reinforcements and would attempt to flank us and get in our rear, thereby preventing our return to New Creek, orders were given to return to New Creek, which was accordingly done.

"The return was made in good order by our troops, but we were closely followed by the rebels in force. A running fight was kept up for a number of miles, without serious results. There was a good deal of artillery firing on both sides, and the booming of rebel cannon in our rear and the explosion of their shells in our midst reminded us that it was unsafe to loiter behind. This was the first action in which the Regiment was engaged and both officers and men behaved splendidly."

Camp Crossman, Newcreek, VA
September 27, 1861.

"Dear Friends,

It was with the greatest of pleasure that I received your excellent letters yesterday. You don't know the pleasure it gives a person to receive letters from friends at home. We are shut out almost from the rest of the world, and a leter is always asceptable. I had thought some time ago that my letters were not asceptable for I had wrote several and received no answers. But the mystery is all cleared up now and I shall try and not have it occur again. I have been over a great deal of Virginia and Maryland since I left Camp Dennison and have been in one skirmish. I shall give you a brief account of it as I presume you have seen an account of it in the papers ere this reaches you. On the 23 inst, 900 Infantry undercommand of Lt. Col. Cantwell with one piece of artillery (6 Pounder) and one Cavalry company, 80 men, left this place for Romney 18 miles distant where the rebels were camped in considerable numbers. We got thereabout 3 o'clock A./M. Tuesday morning. We rested till morning when we divided our force in half, going round to attack them in the rear. The other force failed to meet us and we had to fall back slowly towards New-creek. The enemys force was between two and three thousand with three heavy pieces of artillery. They where strongly intrenched. We brought every thing off safe and took fifteen prisoners. Our loss is five killed and twelve wounded. We have no way of telling what the rebels loss is but have every reason to believe it was heavy. This was my first expierence of a battle and it would be hard to describe my feelings while the bullets were flying around. I felt some slight misgivings at first but was soon over that and had no other feeling throughout the engagement but trying to see how many I could pick off. Thus ended my first engagement. There is no telling how the next one will end. We got to our camp Wednesday night, tired, sore and worn out. Having been gone three days and two nights without any rest. That is one side of soldier life, but it is seldom that we have it as hard as that. I have been in the service over five months and taken all through have had very good times better than I ever expected to have in the army. One reason is I have rather better companions than is generaly found in such places. I shall have to close as I am getting tired. I have written a rough letter but I am ina rough place and according to custom things must accord. Write soon and let me know how all the neighbors are getting along. I should like very much to see you and its likely I shall this winter. I will not come to old Noble again without paying you a visit. Give my best respects to all and keep a large share for yourselves. Goodbye till you hear from me again.

Yours sincerely,
Wm. F. Kimmell
Don't forget to write
PS. I should like one of you to let me know how things are getting along at father's. I sometimes think that things don't go as they should, but I may be mistaken.
W. F. K.

The diary describes the favorite event of the soldier, pay-day. "On the 11th of Oct we got four months wages paid us.It would have done your hearts good to have seen us as we left the pay table with our hard earned cash in our fists and seen the smile of satisfaction as thoughts of home and with what gladness would they hail this our first remittance."

Sawyer's narration continues, "On the 24th day of October the troops again advanced on Romney, the Eighth Regiment being in command of Col. DePuy, who had returned. On the arrival of the troops at Mechanicsburg Gap, the rebels, who had their artillery posted in the Romney cemetery, opened upon them with round shot and shell, but without damage, and it soon becoming evident to Gen. Kelly that this cannonade was for the purpose of covering a retreat, he ordered his column forward. The artillery soon disappeared, and by the time the cavalry reached the village not a rebel soldier was to be seen. The town was now occupied by our troops."

Will's diary on the next day's events, "I was somewhat surprized on the 25th of Oct to be waked up out of a sound sleep and see my father standing before me. I was sorry that his visit was so short. We started for Romney at 12 o'clock the same night. Gen Kelly was our commander.

"26th Oct we stormed the town of Romney after an engagement lasting two hours. The rebels took to their heels. We captured all their camp equipage, four cannon, their spoils that fell into our hands amounted to over $30,000 worth taken all in all. It was one of the most brilliant achievements of the champaign . Our loss did not exceed four men."

In Will's next letter written October 27, 1861 from Romney, he told Leah in detail of the battle at Romney and his feelings about the sight of the dead and wounded on the battle field and of the aid he gave to a fallen soldier comrade.

Romney Virginia
October 27, 1861

Dear Leah,

I hardly feel myself competent to answer your last excellent letter, but I will do my best. I am about tired out and hardly fit to write. We had a warm contest with a supirior force of the rebels at this place yestarday.

We left New-creek about eleven o'Clock Friday night. We marched about eleven miles and stoped till daylight and eat breakfast when we started for this place at three o'clock in the afternoon. We were fired on about two miles from town We soon drove them back and the engagement became general along the river botom. It lasted two hours, when we completely routed them. We captired 25 wagons all loaded down with there equipments. We also took four pieces of artillery. We have more prisoners than we can take care of. Our loss is very small. I have not heard the exact number, but it is not over ten killed and wounded.

I helped bury fifteen rebels today. We buried them all in one grave. Our men are buried seperately. A person never thinks of the dead and wounded during a battle. But it is a horriblle sight after it's all over. During the battle there was one of our men at my right side wounded in the thigh. He fell and called me to help him. I helped him to an ambulance and was at my post again and never thought more of it until the battle was over.

When I went to see him he was in great agony and died last night. Poor fellow. Such is a soldier life.

We are now camped in Romney and we will hold it for a time at least. I had rathe not write of such times but if soldiers did not do it there would not be as m uch writing done in camp today as there is.

Father came to see me last week. He staid one night. I never was more surprised in my life than I was to see him in Va.

If Kate don't write some of this time, well! Wait till I see her again, then she will find out whats the matter. That's all. Don't forget to write soon. If you could only see what pleasure it gives me to get your excellent letters. I have got almost out of the world and I have to watch my chance to get letters to the railroad. You must excuse this poorly written letter. I am to tired altogether to write. Give my Best Respects to all friends.

Good Bye for awhile. Think of me here inthe mountains some times and be assured if I ever fo get wounded, it will not be in the back.

Yours sincerely,
W.F. Kimmell
Direct yours to Newcreek, Va.

The colonel had missed these battles saying in his book that he had been confined to his sick bed at Grafton for over five weeks with typhoid fever, and when able to do so, visited his home at Norwalk, Ohio, but did not sufficiently recover his health to enable him to return to duty until the 29th of October, when he joined his regiment at Romney.

"The country about Romney is hilly and mountainous, and the rebels being in considerable force at Blue's Gap and other points in the vicinity, heavy picketing was required, In a few instances our men were fired upon and some killed by skulking bushwackers."

Will's diary refers to the period after the battle of Romney. "On the afternoon of November 13 we were sent eight miles on the Winchester Road to recover the dead bodies of two Cavalry men that had been shot by the rebels in the morning while on a scout. We succeeded, and returned to camp at ten at night somewhat the worse for ware."

Camp Keyes
Romney, Virginia
November 25, 1861

Dear Leah,

It is with some misgivings that I sit down to answer your very welcome letter that was handed to me this morning. I was out on Picket Guard last night and came in this morning almost froze. One of my mess mates handed me a letter saying, this will warm you up. I looked at the hand writing, broke the seal and read it. He asked is it from home. A little more than from home, I replied. Ah! was the exclamation he made and turned away satisfied.

We have had several snow storms here this fall and the weather is cold, much to cold to live with comfort in our cotton houses and the consequence is bad colds are very prevalent. I have to thank my lucky stars for once that I am a tinker. I found the remains of a rebel tin shop in town and it wasn't long till I had a stove manufactured so hat we are quite comfortable. I still have hopes of getting home this winter if we get into winter quarters I will get to see you without fail and then look out for a good time. If we do not get into winter quarters soon we will be pushed through and if the army is once started this rebellion must soon end and then

I will be free once again. But I am anticipating it may be my fate never to see home nor kind friends again: but

> If now on earth we meet no more
> As we have met in days before
> Still think of me and of the past
> Remember me is all I ask.

I have got a little touch of the blues today and consequently am not quite as lively as usual. It is not my nature to get downhearted, but I do get lonesome at times. I shall quit writing until after dinner and then I will take a fresh start. Tell Bell Vermilyea not to forget to put a stripe down the legs of the first pants she makes for her son. There is no danger of Kate's getting married untill the war is over is their? I reccollect a promise that was once made that I was to be invited to the wedding. I am on a big study what to write. Subjects have got awful scarce with me lately. Everything is so monotinos in camp. When we get moving again I may find something of interest to write and meantime you must expect my letters to be dull. I shall have to bring my scribbling to a close. Give my Best respects to all my friends. Write soon and write often. I always look anxiously for your kind letters. I hope personly to bid you a happy New Years before long, for the present Good Bye.

Yours sincerely
Wm F. Kimmell

Another pay day was noted by W. F. on December 12, 1861. "It did not benefit me a great deal. Col. Depuy and Lt. Col Park resigned. Major Sawyer to Lt. Col, Capt. Winslow to Major and Capt Carroll of the U. S. Regular army was appointed our Col. the regiment is improving every day under him."

Sawyer marks the appointment of Col. S. S. Carroll, of the regular army, as the commanding officer who arrived in camp on December 16. "He was a dashing officer, anxious to distinguish himself and above all to qualify his regiment for its duties. This was a new era in our military life. Col. Carroll was once an authority and a model and we all felt that in the pursuit of the art

military we were no longer groping our way in the dark. Guard duty was brought up to the letter of the army regulations; discipline was strictly enforced; battalion drill regularly required and Sunday morning inspection and dress parade regularly held. The officers subscribed for and procured an elegant silk regimental flag, and in short we found ourselves all at once a well equipped, a well drilled, a plucky and proud regiment."

Will found this new life to be to his liking and describes his life in this manner in his diary, "It may be interesting to give a little account of our camp life. One day is so near like another that I will describe one and it will do for all. At daylight Reville is beat. Then all hands turn out to roll call. The next thing is breakfast. Guns are cleaned up. At ten o'clock drill commences and continues till twelve. Dinner at half past twelve. Drill from two to four. At half past four we have dress parade. Then supper. At eight o'clock tattoo is beat, then the roll is called. Half past eight the taps are sounded. Then all lights are put out and everything becomes quite. This is a soldiers every day life in camp.

"Christmas was a very dull day in camp. All the difference between it and other day's was there was no drilling done...We fixed up our camp so that it had a very plesent look. We planted a row of evergreen trees in front of each line of tents forming streets between each company. The white tents and green trees forming a very pleasent contrast. New Years passed away the year 1861 with the 8th Reg O. V. I., U. S. A."

The year 1862 began for the 8th Ohio with the command to be in readiness to march and so on the 6th of January, Sawyer states, "we had three days cooked rations and forty rounds of ammuntion. This looked like a fight and the men were jubliant. The objective point was Blue's Gap, it having been determined to drive out the Bushwhackers who had of late become very troublesome from that point. Soon after dark the detachment moved out; there was snow on the ground and the night was clear and cold. We came in sight of the Gap at daylight next morning, when the Fourth and Fifth Regiments were deployed forward up the mountains and the Eighth ordered to charge through the Gap, which was done most spiritedly."

Will's diary records the battle, "Col. Carroll was the first man to enter the Gap, and set fire to the mill. The rebels took to there heels after the first fire leaving two cannon and all the camp equipage in our hands. They left nine dead bodies on the ground. We did not loose a man. We removed all their property of value and destroyed the remainder."

Sawyer continues his narrative, "An artist was 'on the spot' and sketched the scene which was produced in some of the New York pictorials. It was ascertained that no considerable number of troops had ever been stationed there, but it had for a long time been the rendezvous of a gang of Bushwackers. We returned to Romney in the evening, tired, cold and hungry, but quite pleased to have been in a battle and to have come through safely. A heavy mail went out the next day, carrying curious and flaming accounts of the sanguinary battle of Blue's Gap."

The troops had now been furnished with Sibley tents. "They were pitched on lodge poles, and afforded very comfortable quarters for the men. The officers had generally the wall tent, or occupied buildings about town. Good stables had been built for the animals, and we began to feel comfortably fixed up for the winter. Our tents were new and comfortable, rations abundant, and varied at times with turkey and chickens that some how straggled into town with wagon-master "Jonathan's " forage train. The people were civil to us, especially as Gen Kelley issued an order that we should pay the master for services of his slave.

"Gen F. W. Lander arrived on the 9th of January with orders to take command and fall back to the line of the rail road. Our trunks and extra baggage were at once sent off to Cumberland (Maryland), and all the teams about the country taken possession of by the quartermaster, to aid in transporting the camp and garrison equipage, much of which, including some tents had to be burnt.

"On the evening of the 10th, everything was in readiness, and the troops moved out about eleven o'clock, and marched some twelve miles, when we halted, and although very cold, lay down on the snow and slept soundly for three or four hours. The fact, that Stonewall Jackson's force was said to be in motion, somewhere between us and Winchester, led to the belief that we might be attacked, and this point had been selected by Gen Lander for a fight, if it was offered.

Scouts who had been sent out reported no force within reach and our march was resumed. The eighth acted as skirmishers on right flank. By noon it began to rain. The roads were heavy and the streams swollen, and the march consequently slow. We arrived at Patterson's Creek, at its confluence with the Potomac a little after dark. Our wagon master had our tents up and our mess boys and strikers had prepared for our hungry condition, with chickens and other good things, accumulated along the wagon route.

"A very sad thing happened this evening. Our muskets had been loaded and capped, during the march, as we were on the right flank, where an attack was probable and the men coming into camp tired and wet, laid down their arms wherever convenient, while arranging their quarters. Some soldier carelessly took hold of a gun to remove it, when it went off, killing John Smith, of Co. 3, instantly."

WF writing to his friend, George (no further identification) from Cumberland, Maryland, January 14, 1862, describes the march in this manner,

"I have plenty time this evening and will try and scribble you a few lines. We have got away from Romney at last and a most awful hard march we had of it. We left Romney Friday night. It was raining all day Friday and you can imagine how marching went. We got here Saturday evening after pulling through the mud for twenty miles. We are now on the railroad eight miles below Cumberland. We will not stay here but a short time. This move was made to catch the rebel Gen (Jackson) but he was to quick for us and escaped. Our march nearly killed me. Today was the first time I have been out. I will be all right again in a day or two. You must excuse me for not writing more this time. I will do better after this. Direct to Cumberland MD and write on evelope, please forward to Regt. Give my respects to all friends

Truly yours,
W. F. Kimmell

Sawyer continued his story of the march to Cumberland with these remarks, "The picket duty was pretty severe, as our line extended out on the rail road several miles, and round to the ford on Patterson's Creek, four miles from camp and thence along the Knobelly mountains to near Cumberland. On the 15th the troops were brigaded. The Fourth, Fifth and Eighth Ohio and thirty-ninth Illinois composing the Second brigade; what was called a 'straight regulation review' was had on the 17th. All of us who had them, came out with our epaulets and regulation hats, and we believed ourselves to have come fully up to the standard of the regular McClellan reviews in front of Washington."

The next letter written to Leah and Kate was datelined Camp Kelly, January 15th, 62.

"Dear Friend Leah,
I received your welcome letter with three others today and least I should not have a chance of answering it soon, I will do it right away. I was glad to hear that you enjoyed yourself during the hollidays. We got our goose roasted on Christmas and I

don't suppose we were as long eating it as you were with yours. We have had a very hard march from Romney here. We left there Friday night. The mud was shoe top deep so that we had a plesent little walk of twenty miles. It is froze up very hard with considerable snow on the ground. We have the large Sibley Tents and a stove in each and we have plenty to eat. What more does a soldier want. But still I would like to attend some of your spelling schools and parties. I came near forgetting to mention that I have been in a skirmish lately. Your probably have seen it mentioned in the papers. It was at a place called Blue Gap, fifteen miles east of Romney. I came very near having a stop put to my career then. There was a bullet went through my coat. A miss is as good as a mile any time.

Give my respects to all friends and keep the largest share for yourself and now kind friend, Good Bye for the present.

From your true friend
W. F. Kimmell

Direct to Cumberland, MD.

Dear Friend Kate,

I was glad to hear from you again as I always am to hear from friends. I have written four letters today and am getting very tired. I have not been well for several days. I caught a very heavy cold on our march from Romney here. It rather got the better of me, but I am nearly well again.

I am sorry that I could not spend the holliday at home. I hope in another year that we will all be at home. Write again.

Truly yours,
WFK

"On the 22nd," Sawyer said,, "a reconnaissance of the rail road as far as the Little Capucon was made. We had an engine and cars sufficient for two companies, while the other two were deployed on the front and right flank, the Potomac river covering the left flank to prevent surprise. At French's store , we found a large quantity of rebel corn, which was taken possession of and next day carried to camp and used for forage. The RR track was found but little disturbed and on this report, Gen. Landers had parties out repairing it, the next day, preparatory to moving down river."

On February 2nd, WFK wrote to Leah from Camp Kelly, Cumberland Maryland.

Dear Leah,

I was truly happy to hear from you again. It found me in good health with the exception of a very disagreeable cold. It is very hard for a soldier to get rid of a cold.

We have some snow on the ground but no sleighing. I have seen no good sleighing this winter. The last sleigh ride I had was the last time I saw you. I should like very much to have another just like it. I do hope by another winter to enjoy it. This unnatural war cannot last much longer, everything points towards a speedy close, but if it should last longer than three years, I shall enlist again. The ending of this war will be the ending of slavery. I hope they will not be freed and allowed to live in the United States. It would never do to put them on an equality with the whites. The way that works is to be seen here in the army. When we first went to Romney there was a number of slaves joined us. We get them to work for us, then they would do anything for us. As soon as they saw that we treated them as equals, they got saucy, impudent and do all the mischief they could. At last they got unbearable and we had to run them out of the army.

We moved our camp yesterday about a mile to get out of the mud. We are now camped in a very pleasent situation.

I am afraid that Kate and you quarrel sometimes about your arrangements. I should like very much to be invited to Kate's wedding but I am afraid it will be yours first.

Mrs. Haas writes me that it is whispered in the neighborhood that Mr. Foot is paying his addresses to Miss Leah C., but you say it is Kate and I am bound to believe you. If there is a wedding goes off, let me know in time and I may possibly be there.

You must excuse this very poor letter. I can handle the Rifle a great deal better than the pen. Write again soon. Tell me all the news about everything and everybody. Thanking you for your good wishes, I still remain your true friend.

Will Direct co Cumberland

On the 9th of February, the troops began to move after having fixed the railroad and they went by cars to PawPaw Tunnel. Sawyer describes this location , "This is a point where the Ohio and Chesapeake Canal passes through a tunnel under a spur of the Cacupon Mountains, and also the railroad. The scenery was beautiful, but our camps are so wretched that we had but little disposition to admire the grand scenery.

"We were constantly being harassed by bushwhackers whose headquarters were said to be at Bloomey Gap, some twenty miles distant. So about noon of the 15th, General Lander, at the head of the eight regiments of infantry started to raid the Bloomey. The swollen and cold Little Cacupon river and the Cacupon mountains had to be crossed. The engineer corps was utterly puzzled as to any means of bridging the stream. Our wagonmaster, "Jonathan" informed the general that he had been "engineer corps" with a circus for some years and he thought that he could apply the same principles he used then to putting the army across in about an hour. He hitched a good stout span of mules to a wagon tongue with plenty of ballast in the wagon, and drove through the river to the opposite bank and then detaching the mules, another and another wagon hauled and left tandem, until the river was spanned when boards were thrown on top and the troops soon crossed.

"We marched rapidly all night, and arrived at the Gap just at daylight . With some cavalry, Lander dashed up a ravine and into the headquarters of a Col. Baldwin, the commandant of the post, who with his staff still snugly in bed and minus uniform were captured in their night gowns."

Sawyer stated that because the union troops would not take advantage of their position, the rebels got away. "In this skirmish two of our cavalry were killed, and one or two wounded and several horses killed. Of the rebels, seven officers, including Col Baldwin and about twenty men were captured.

"We returned to camp during the afternoon, a good deal wearied and worn, but were soon amply compensated for our toil by the glowing accounts in the papers of the spirited 'battle of Bloomey Gap'."

Shortly after this, General Lander withdrew the troops and the rebels again secured the bridge and burned it. Col. Carroll sent a detachment of the 8th back to repair the bridge. This time a guard was left to protect it.

Will wrote to Kate and Leah again from Maryland on the 23rd of February.

"Dear Leah,

It was with the greatest of pleasure that I again heard of your welfare. I do not know what would become of us soldiers if it were not for the cheering letters of our friends. You had ought to be here at mail time and see us. The whole company are after the captain enquiring for letters. It would be a study for a Phrenologist to see the different expressions on our faces as the answers are returned. Some smiling, some half mad and some hopeful. As I have a good many correspondents, I get plenty of letters, but none do I look for as anxious as my best of friends. (I will leave you to guess who.)

I was glad to know that you took those few lines in my last as a joke. I assure you that nothing else was intended. I ought not to have written Mrs. Haas news had it been any body else but you I should not have done it. We will let it drop as it is. We have been friends long enough to be perfectly acquainted and I hope no quarrel may ever arise to mar our friendship. I have strong hopes of being home by the fourth of July if our arms meet with the success thay have for the past month, I certainly shall.

We are laying here anxious to be led on to the enemy as we are fighting men from Gen. Lander down to the lowest private in the ranks. You will hear an account of the eighth Ohio worth reading.

We had a recent skirmish at Bloomey Gap. You will find an account of it in this letter.

When I get home I am going to place myself under your hand for a month to tame so you can make up your mind for a hard customer.

You must excuse this poor writing. This is the best pen that I can lay hands on.

There is no proper word that will express how miserable it is. So you may know nearly how it is.

Your absent friend,

Will

Direct as before
Good Night

Dear Friend Kate,

As usual I was very happy to hear from you. I certainly would rather see you than to write, but that is the best we can do and in time of war we must be satisfied.

I am afraid the war will be ended before I get another chance at the rebels. I do want a few more good shots and I will be satisfied that I have done my share in this rebellion. If I were not to get into another battle, I never would be satisfied. I have thought I never want to go in another battle, but I have got tired of doing nothing.

I must close, Bidding you good Bye for the present. Give my respect to friends.
Yours in friendship,
W. F. Kimmell

———

According to Co. Sawyer, the 8th began their move on to Winchester on the first day of March. "Gen. Lander was in feeble health but was expected to join the Regiment the next day. It was very cold, and the men, having no tents and but few blankets, suffered greatly. In the morning it began to snow and soon the ground was covered. We remained in our position until 2 o'clock when we began to retrace our steps and soon after we learned that Gen. Lander was dead. He had suffered a heart attack. After our return we remained in camp, except the picket details.

"On the fifth of March we broke up camp, and moved by rail to Sir John's Run, where we built fires, breakfasted and remained until night when the railroad being patched up, we moved up to Back Creek,. We camped here for the night and the railroad ended. The bridge across the Creek at this point had been destroyed and not rebuilt. The next morning we marched toward Martinsburg, some sixteen miles away. Our horses did not arrive so we were compelled to make the march on foot. We crossed the creek on a rope bridge, and over the most miserable roads, we finally arrived at Martinsburg. The teams had gone around and were on hand at our arrival with tents and provisions so the the tired hungry soldiers were soon settled for a night's rest.

"We moved toward Winchester on the 11th and came upon Gen. Banks during the night. We lay on our arms till daylight. We expected to assault the enemy in the morning. We watched the line until it entered and passed the enemies out works, and until news came back that the enemy had left. A battle being out of the question, we were dismissed to our rations of chickens, hams, etc., picked up by foraging parties. We went into camp on the north end of Winchester. At this point Gen. James Shields assumed command of our division which was during our stay in the valley, known as Shields division.

"Here the division was re-brigaded. The 4th & 8th Ohio & 67th Ohio, 14th Indiana and Seventh Virginia. These remained during their entire term of service, and became one of the best and most celebrated of the Potomac Army."

Will described these events in his letter to Leah written from the new camp area near Winchester.

Fort Hill, Winchester, VA
March 21st, 1862

Dear Leah,

Your kind letter of the 10th just reached me last night. We have been moving so much lately that our mail has been very uncertain. We started from Pawpaw on the first day of March for Winchester and marched 12 miles and stopped for the night. The next day we were ordered back. Gen Lander's death was the reason of our being recalled. On the 5th we started by rail for Martinsburg. We came to within 10 miles of the place. There the bridge over Back Creek being destroyed, the rest of the way had to be marched. The baggage was left behind and I was left in charge and did not get to the Regt untill day before yesterday. The Regt started from Martinsburg for Winchester on the 11th. On the 12th they entered the town without firing a gun. Our Division (Gen Shields) left here for Strausburg to rout the rebels and succeeded perfectly. We was gone three days, had two skirmishes, marched 64 miles, got back all safe, but was nearly wore out.

When you read an account of it in the paper there will be an honorable mention made of the Eighth Regt and its gallant Col. Carroll.

This rebellion cannot last much longer. Every day we hear of the success of the union arms. Yestarday we got the news of Gen Burnside's victory at Newberne, N.C. It is impossible for the rebels to hold out much longer. Jeff Davis will soon be trying to find his way to Europe. We will all be home by the 4th of July or I am no prophet.

You are right in saying that slavery ought to be removed, and when it is removed, the slaves must be taken out of the country. It will never do to free tham and have them among us as equals. I am not abolitionist enough to think a Negro as good as a white man. President Lincoln's plan of buying the negros and colonizing them suits me the best of anything that I have saw yet.

My respects to Kate. I am sorry she did not have time to write. I shall be happy to receive that invitation, but am afraid that I can't be there. Write all the perticulars and I will have to be satisfied.

As I can think of nothing else worth writing of, I will close. When you answer direct to Winchester, VA. Give my best respects to all friends and now kind friend, adieu for the present. Sometimes think of you absent soldier friend

W. F. Kimmell

Excuse my poor writing, I am to tired to write with any satisfaction. I have been trying hard to fill up this sheet but I am not going to succeed, that's all.

Col. Sawyer continues his tale by saying that General Shields had led a reconnaissance in force up the valley to determine the strength of the enemy. He sent the 8th with one company of the 4th Ohio and Clark's battery, starting at three in the morning, and moved by a circuitous route to cut off an enemy retreat toward Front Royal and of seizing the bridge at Strasburg.

"Before our arrival at Strasburg, the rebels had made safe their retreat. We found the bridge in flames and the enemy posted with his artillery on a hill on the other side and from which he opened fire on the head of our column. Clark ran his battery forward, the writer supported with three companies of the 8th and Col. Carroll deployed the balance of the regiment along the bank of the river as sharp-shooters and skirmishers. Two of our cavalry were wounded, but no other damage

"After dark we withdrew to a dense cedar grove to the right of the road and bivouacked for the night. During the night a temporary bridge was constructed across Cedar Creek and as soon as daylight appeared the artillery opened fire and our advance troops commenced to cross. The rebels retreated rapidly. We passed one dead rebel, literally cut in two by a cannon ball."

The leaders determined that this rebel force was under command of Ashby, the terror and the wizard of the Shenandoah. Col. Sawyer stated that "He was represented as being always mounted on a white horse, of being everywhere present, and of wearing a charmed life." Consequently everything astride a white horse in front, in rear, along the mountains near at hand or in the distance, was at once conjured up in the minds of the soldier to be Ashby. His apparition had presented itself frequently during the day, evening and morning, and still hovered about fitfully in the advance.

"The troops advanced into Strasburg and took a position on a hill overlooking the country to the south, while the cavalry wound around among the mountains in pursuit of Ashby. Col. Daum seeing the head of this line emerge from a glen at some distance, ordered Capt. Clark to fire into it, believing it to be Ashby. Clark yelled at him, stating that this was our own men, but finally, yielding to the commander, he shot. The result was two of our own men wounded and three horses killed.

"Friendly Fire"

"The entire forces crossed the ravine and formed on the opposite bank. Col. Carroll led the 8th himself, leading the left wing and Sawyer the right. We soon saw the white horse and rider up the hill and the closer we got, we saw that there were two pieces of artillery with him. Another and another shot passed in close proximity. Our skirmishers began to fire and in the twinkling of an eye, Ashby, white horse and artillery were dashing up the road and away with commendable speed.

"We returned to Strasburg and took possession of a church, sheds and enjoyed a night's rest, returning to camp the next morning in a drenching rain and over terrible roads."

The next battle of some consequence was the battle of Winchester which occured on the 22nd of March. The entire 8th Regiment was involved in this and with considerable loss to the group.

"Before getting into position, two of Gen. Shield's horses were killed by the explosion of a shell, a fragment of which struck the general on the left arm and broke it. The Regiment pushed forward rapidly as skirmishers soon drove the rebel battery and its supports back on Kearnstown; and after a half hours skirmishing, all was quiet. We lay on our arms, in line, all night, but were not molested. The next morning, as all was quiet, Col Carroll started back to Martinsburg, to bring his family from there to Winchester. Our tents were brought and we set up camp.

"About ten o'clock the picket lines were again attacked, and the artillery opened briskly. The 8th was again ordered to the front as skirmishers, and by the time we had got under arms, Col Carroll returned and took command.

"The rebels soon directed a heavy cannonade at this point, their shell plunging down among us, but fortunately with little damage. Stonewall Jackson with a force of about eight thousand men, was in our front and expected to take tea with friends in Winchester, a fact that the town ladies boasted about throughout the day."

According to Col. Sawyer, a fierce fight ensued throughout the day. As he said, cannon balls were crashing through the trees fearfully close. "We were separated from the rebels by a rail fence, which was nearly demolished. The fight was almost hand to hand, some of the men discharging and then clubbing their muskets.

"The fire from both sides was intense, our men fell rapidly but gallantly held their places, loading rapidly and firing with unerring certainty, as the dead in front plainly showed. The rebels held out for about thirty minutes when they broke and ran. The rout being complete we received orders to fall back.

"This was really our first battle. It has seldom been the fate of troops to suffer greater loss in any engagement, over one-fourth of my command were killed and wounded. My horse was struck twice and my sash pierced with a ball. I tried to send my horse down into a ravine and he refused to go, but persistently followed wherever I went. During the night the dead were buried and wounded sent back to Winchester."

 W.F. described this in his letters to Leah and Kate datelined Woodstock, Virginia, April 15, 1862.

Dear Leah,

I was very happy to hear from you once again. It is so seldom that I get a letter, when I do get one it is so much the more welcome.

The verses are excellent and I shall preserve them. You have no idea how much it cheers us soldiers to receive words of encouragement from friends at home. In going into battle thoughts of what our friends would say if we are defeated is enough of itself to make us strive for the victory.

I was in the battle in which Gen Shields was wounded. He was at the head of our Regt at the time he was hit. He is a brave man, and his me all love him. He has been with us almost ever since the battle. That is something that very few men would do in his situation.

You wanted me to give you accounts of the battles I am in. It will give me great pleasure to do so. I am keeping a diary and if I once get time to put it in readable shape I will send it to you. I will not attempt in this letter to give you any acocunt of the Battle of Winchester.

I had my wish gratified with regard to shooting the rebels somewhat sooner than I expected. I fired over twenty shots at lessthan fifty yards ad I think not without doing the union cause some service. I had four bullet hoes in my overcoat, one of them give me a little scratch on the arm.

If I could go home tomorrow and stay, I would not do it. I enlisted with the intension of seeing it through and I shall stay intil peace is restored once more in our now distracted country. And I still think it will be in time for us to celebrate the 4th of July at home. I will not close hoping to hear from you soon again. Write to Winchester for the present.

Good Bye
W.F. KImmell
In The Army April 15

Friend Kate

I was surprised when I read your letter for I realy expected to hear of a wedding. You think you are to old to marry. But their has been older people than you have been married before today, but I suppose I must be saisfied with it as it is.

You wished to be excused from writing every time, although I would wish very mucyh to hear from every letter, but if it is not convenient for you to do so, I certainly cannot ask it of you. But write whenever you can. Excuse my writing.

Truly yours,
W.F.Kimmell

During this time period the 8th Ohio was involved in engagements at Woodstock, Edinburg, Mt. Jackson, and Harrisonburg while in pursuit of Stonewall Jackson. But the 8th did have time to enjoy the country side as Col. Sawyer stated, "This campaign in the Shenandoah Valley introduced us to one of the fairest parts of the earth. The country is rich and productive. The wooded mountains to the west, and the incomparable outline of the Blue Ridge to the east, make up a panorama of the rarest beauty.

"On the 12 of May, the division of Gen Shields was detached from Bank's command, and commenced its march to join Gen. McDowell's force at Fredericksburg. Gen Shields thought that but a small rebel force remained in the valley. Gen Banks believed that Jackson was watching a favorable opportunity to retake the valley. Banks argued that the forces should not be depleted and predicted disastrous consequences.

"We left camp at seven enjoying the beautiful day and scenery. The baggage train and extra horses, provisions and other comforts of camp life had improved vastly of late. All of this shed a favorable influence over the troops. About ten o'clock on the morning of the 14th as we neared Front Royal we heard a train whistle which was cause for celebration by the entire division since the men had not heard this sound since we left Back Creek.

"We remained at Front Royal for two days when we commenced our march up the Blue Ridge by way of Chester Gap. We then moved to Catlett's Station, left on the 21st and reached Falmouth, opposite Fredericksburg. On the 23rd, our division was reviewed on the plain in front of the Lacy House by President Lincoln, Secretary Stanton, and Gen. McDowell.

"Col. Carroll received a nomination as Brigadier General and the division was re-brigaded, leaving four regiments to a brigade. This nomination was never confirmed until the close of our three years, yet Col. Carroll was never returned to duty with his regiment and the command evolved unto the writer."

"On the evening of the 24th, information was received of the defeat of Gen. Banks in the valley and of his rapid retreat into Maryland. Consequently the division was ordered to move at three o'clock in the morning. The men were greatly disappointed, as they had believed they were in full march to Richmond, to realize the hanging of Jeff Davis on a sour apple tree, and now to be turned back with haste to the north, and to have to retake the valley was very disheartening to both officers and men."

According to Sawyer the troops returned to the valley and within four miles of Manassas Junction they went into camp. "We passed the remains of the old rebel camp at Manassas where we saw the perfect specimens of the frightful 'quaker gun' (the rebels cut down trees and made them appear to be cannon) and a drove of negroes, mostly women and children, who had been left behind when camp was broken up. We passed a camp where we found swords, pistols, tents, beds and officer's clothing showing a very hasty retreat. We arrived at Rectortown on the 28th from which we could see the out-posts of the rebels near Front Royal.

"We dashed into Front Royal and took three hundred prisoners, and released about four hundred prisoners of a cavalry regiment and other troops who had been captured a few days before by the rebels. Among our prisoners was the celebrated Belle Boyd.(Famous confederate woman spy.)

"The march to Winchester continued through rain and floods. On the morning of June 1st we heard cannonade in the direction of Strassburg and felt that Fremont was upon the Jackson forces."

Col. Sawyer reported that after several days fighting, Jackson had escaped from Fremont and was rapidly consummating one of the most brilliant movements of the war. "For the last ten days the rain had fallen constantly and in torrents. The roads were heavy and the streams and marshes overflowed and swollen, yet before Gen. Shields was aware of the movement, Jackson had marched six to eight miles in scarcely the same number of hours and was absolutely behind the Chickahominy and on McClellan's flank, and powerfully demonstrating to that officer the necessity of a change of base.

"In consequence of his late conduct Shields was relieved of his command and was not heard of again during the war.

"Our brigade moved slowly back to Luray, where we remained several days, and where we got paid. On the 21st we commenced to fall back from Luray, and on the 24th, after a severe march, reached Bristoe Station, on the Orange and Alexandria Railroad, where we went into camp and remained until the 28th, when we were transported to Alexandria by railroad and from thence to Harrison's Landing, on James river by steamboat."

Will's comments about this time period were in a letter he wrote to Leah from Bristoe Station.

June 25, 1862

Dear Friend

I received your letter of June 8th yesterday it found me well as usual. I was sorry to know that you were troubled with a headache at the time of writing, but that don't last always. It was just two days of being one month since we camped at this place before. Since then we have marched two hundred and ten miles and part of our division had a sever battle at Port Republic. Our brigade (1st) were not in the action. Although we had a little skirmish in covering the retreat of our men. This has been the hardest march we have had yet. From Luray we marched day and night -over the worst road in the country in order to head of Jackson's army from crossing the Shanandoah river, but we were one day to late.

So we had our trouble for our pains. On our march back for three days we had no provisions and half of us were without shoes. But it is all over now and we will have good times. Unless something unusual turns up. We are going to Washington City to rest and recruit. If there is any possible chance to get a leave of absence I will be home. But I am afraid there will be no chance. Unless the battle at Richmond should be decided in our favor.

We are now camped on the Orange and Alexandia Rail-Road three miles south of Manassas Junction.

I saw Henry Hardenburg yesterday. He sends his best respects to Kate and yourself. He is in the second Brigade.

I have so many letters to write this morning that I will have to make them all short, if we have the good luck to get to Washington I will try and get time to write a readable letter. Untill then Good-Bye. I still remain your ever since friend.

Will
Direct same as before

Shortly after Will wrote the above letter the Regiment was on the move again. This time they went to Alexandria by rail and then onto Harrison's Landing on the James River where they embarked on steamboats. Col. Sawyer mentions that the men enjoyed their steamboat excursions. "They noticed the great historic points along the Potomac, Mt. Vernon and scenes of Colonial and Revolutionary events.

"The next night we dropped anchor in Hampton Roads and saw the Fortress Monroe, the rip-raps and the masts of the Cumberland, still remaining as left, when sunk by the rebel iron clad.

On July first the group started up the James River feeling somewhat depressed since learning " what McClellan's change of base meant, and the causes therefor. The fate of his army was now in great doubt, the most appalling disasters being feared."

The Brigade was involved in fights at Malvern Hill and Turkey Bend. Sawyer continues his narrative "On the morning of the 4th, the glorious Fourth of July, we were aroused by a scattering fire along the picket line, and a road passing through and at right angles with the line, was completely enfiladed by artillery and sharp shooters." One of the troopers from Company C, (a

German immigrant) who was taking Sawyer's horses to water discovered the rebels when he was shot at by them, hurried back to camp, lying low on the horse's backs yelling, "Meshter Colonel, It ish no goot going down dare."

Sawyer said that this several hour skirmishing resulted in the rebels establishing a strong picket line and "leaving seven men in the Eighth wounded, two mortally; so ended our Fourth of July."

Several days constant severe fighting left the men without food or good treatment for their wounds. A great deal of sickness was in the camp.

"We were in the midst of most interesting scenes of our early colonial history. The home of Benjamin Harrison, the ruins of old Jamestown , the Westover Estate, home of the famous Byrd family. Our constant duties prevented us from being paid on time, so, the muster was had on the 12 th of July. Our camp was changed to a more central position and on the 22nd, we were re-viewed by General McClellan and he commented on our duties at the front. From then until the 16th of August we remained at this post and our duties were the usual routine of a military camp.

"A Richmond paper was circulated about our location and its fitness for a Yankee camp. We appreciated its comment about Harrison's Landing that there was no place known to geography, and but one to theology hotter than Harrison's Landing."

The Regiment was on the move again, passing through President John Tyler's farm, crossed the Chickahominy by means of a pontoon bridge, and on the 18th found green corn abundant for the men and continued marching until the 20th of August when the corps arrived at Yorktown. They then passed through Williamsburg on to Hampton and arrived again at Newport News where they went into camp.

On August 25th the corps received orders to move again. " We embarked on the ocean steamer, the Cahawba, a large fine ship. We weighed anchor at daylight, steamed down the river and entered Chesapeake Bay. We arrived at Alexandria on August 28 and moved out in front of Fairfax Landing and went into camp. That is, camp without tents, camp garrison or any other equipage except our arms and knapsacks.

"All this time we heard of disaster to Pope's army. On the 29th, our entire corps being now united, moved back through Alexandria and up the river where we bivouacked in front of the Arlington House, in full view of the city of Washington—it appeared to be safe.
"The terrible disaster of 'the second Bull Run' was know known to everyone. The road was full of splendid carriages from Washington being rapidly driven to the battlefield to serve as ambulances, while wagons and ambulances were pouring past us with the wounded and dying to places of safety."

Sawyer commented that the Regiment participated in the fight at Centreville and on up to the right of the Gainesville Pike where they did not see any evidence of battle. In the lull of battle many of the officers rode out to see if anyone could give some account of the fate of the Ohio troops. "We found Capt. Taber of the 55th Ohio, struggling through the streets of town with a mule train. The Ohio troops had suffered severely, especially in the last battle.

"McClellan and his generals came in for a good share of censure and curses at every point. A Col. Gavins of the 14th Indiana asked Gen Milroy (a pious and devout man) the cause of this terrible defeat. 'Treachery and incompetency, by G—.

"We occupied our position until Aug,. 31 when General Phil Kearney and Gen. Stevens came by on their way to attack a rebel force near Fairfax. The distant hum of musketry was all but drowned in the fury of a rain storm which flooded the whole country and completely drenched every thread of our garments. We knew of the activity with which the retreat was going on by the noise and cursing of the teamsters, and the smoke from the burning of equipage, disabled wagons and ambulances.

"As we passed over the plains to the pike road, we discovered the whole surface trodden into a mire. Men sunk in the mud and lost their places. The ditches on either side of the road were literally filled with the remains of burning wagons, caissons overset and abandoned. Surgical instruments were strewn along the road, medicine chests, arms knapsacks, blankets and overcoats.

"The march was slow and wearisome. We breakfasted near Fairfax Court House and watched the solemn procession bearing the bodies of Phil Kearney and Gen. Stevens. We formed a line near Germantown and although the rebels shelled us our batteries replied. The day became pleasant and the men rested. Then the Regiment was formed on the right flank, the most remote from the enemy. Other troops complained and we were transferred to the left, the exposed flank. We crossed over the Potomac by the Chain Bridge into Maryland and went into camp."

According to Sawyer's record the Regiment was camped here and received pay. Then the marching began again, moving about five miles a day. They moved to Clarksburg, Frederick City (a most beautiful town). Sawyer said that the ladies waved handkerchiefs and banners. He thought they might have seen Barbara Fritchie. The men were wild with enthusiasm not having seen a woman that wore a smile in over a year.

The Brigade marched and fought over a great deal of territory and on the morning of the 16th began the fight at Antietam.

"What a day," continues Sawyer, "Nearly half of the officers and men of the Eighth were killed and wounded, and the loss in the balance of the brigade was equally appalling. The men complained that their guns were foul or their ammunition exhausted. The ground was covered with arms along the field and the men were ordered to change their pieces for these and the officers went about picking up and distributing ammunition."

The narrative continued about the fight and the terrible loss on both sides. Sawyer stated that 162 officers and men had been killed and wounded, or about half the number engaged. The loss in other regiments was equally severe, but the brigade had achieved undying renown. It had taken and held one of the most difficult and important positions on the field, and had maintained an unwavering line during the carnage of a four hours' battle. Gen. Sumner pronounced it the 'Gibraltar Brigade.' The barn on the Roulett farm was used for an operating room and the ground about it was covered with wounded and dying men.

The men were sent out to Harper's Ferry on the morning of the 22nd of September. "We forded the Potomac just above the railroad bridge, and passing through the village of

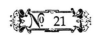

Harper's Ferry, went into camp on Bolivar Heights. The next day our tents arrived and our camps were regularly laid out and tents pitched. This was the first we had seen of them since leaving the Peninsula. Our rest was sweet indeed."

Will's story continues with his letter to Leah from Bolivar Heights on October 16, 1862.

Bolivar Heights Near Harpers Ferry
October 16, 1862

My Dear Friend,

It has been a long, long, time since I last received a letter from you. Why it is I cannot tell. Our mail has been very irregular for the past two months. That may be the reason.

The last letter I received from you was a short time before we left Harrisons Landing. I answered it , and also wrote you from Georgetown, D. C. so that this makes the third since I received one from you. but you may have written as many and more for aught I know. So I shall say no more about it. We have experienced the hardest times in the last two months that it has yet been our lot yet to endure. We have been on the march continualy. And have taken an active part in two of the severest battles of the war. Our company lost heavily at the battle of Antietam. Four killed and sixteen wounded out of the thirty-two engaged. How I ever escaped unharmed is a mystery to me. But my turn will come soon enough if they keep on a few months longer as they have been doing.

We came into Virginia fifteen months ago with one hundred and three men in the company. Today we can muster but twenty-four men for duty.

It is a sad picture to look back over the past and think of they many once happy homes that have been made desolate, And Why. All on account of a few miserable Fanatics both North and South. And then to think the war is no nearer to a conclusion (except in the lapse of time) than it was ten months ago.

Leah, I am almost in dispair of the war ever ending if they keep carrying it on in the way they have been doing. Our Government has never been in earnest. Why are they continualy haggling about a few dispisable Negros. If slavery is in the way why is it not removed by the quietest means in our power.

Our Government treats the south to much like the old man in the Fable trying to make the boy come down off the apple tree by throwing grass at him. They ought to know by this time that the South is in earnest. And using every way and means in their power to gain their independence. Why not meet them in the same way. Not heed their threats let them raise the black flag if they wish to. And see how long they will exist as an army.

Let this army once see that this Government and its Generals are in earnest. And it will be worth a hundred thousand men to them. This is a pretty strong letter, but I have written just as I feel, and I am not the only one (by far) that has the same opinions.

The weather is changing to winter very fast, almost to fast for our comfort, but it will not be long untill we move father south. Part of our Forces started this morning, and we may follow in a few hours. This is a long letter for me to write and I am in hopes that it will bring me an answer right speedily. Give my particular respects to Kate and all friends that may enquire after me.

Most truly your Sincere Friend
W. F. Kimmell Direct to Co. C., 8th Ohio Regt.
Frenches Division Harpers Ferry Virginia

Leah had answered Will shortly after the above letter and he responded with a letter to her datelined November 5th written near Upperville, VA in which he described more of camp life.

Nov 5th 1862

My Dear Friend,
Your excellent letter of Oct 26th I received while at dinner today. I was about as hungry as a Soldier usualy gets, but I could not wait to eat my dinner. The letter had to be read first. It had been so long since I heard from you that I didn't know but you might have been married and left the country. Still there is not much danger of that while the war lasts. Young men are to scarce.

I will tell you what we had for diner and you can judge how we live. We had sweet potatoes, fresh pork, hard crackers and coffee and I dare say that I enjoyed it as much as we ever did a dinner at home.

I have learnt how to be a considerable of a cook. I can bake a good pie, clean and roast a chicken as quick and good as the best of them.

I don't wonder at Billy (Crispell, Leah's brother) wanting to get home to get something good to eat. Army Rations are not very palatable food for a sick person. I knew while I was sick in the Hospital at Camp Dennison my only cry was for something good to eat. It will get harder with Billy because he has always been at home and had some person to take care of him. I have got so used to Pork & Beans and Hard crackers that I scarcely every wish for any thing else.

The weather is getting to be very severe. It is pleasant marching through the day, but the nights are a little to frosty to sleep comfortable. We carry no tents with us. Last night three of us slept under one blanket as I had the middle I slept comfortable enough but my hair was frozen so stiff this morning that I had to hold my head over the fair ten minutes before I could comb it. You wanted a copy of my diary. I will not be able to fulfill any promise because I have lost it. It was in my knapsack at the Battle of Antietam. In making a charge I threw it off so as not to be encumbered. When I went to look for it, it wasn't there. I wouldn't have lost it for a good deal as I had taken great pains to keep it correct.

I still have your miniature, but I have carried it in my pack so long that it is almost worn out. I should like very much to have another. If you have one that you would send in a letter as well as not. But don't put yourself to any trouble to send one. I will send you one of mine in this. It is a poorly taken picture. When you write again let me know how Kate is getting along. Also Bell and the rest of the neighbors. You need never stop writing for fear that I can't read it all. I never have any trouble in doing that. Send me Billy's address and I will write him a letter. You did send it once but I have forgotten it. Give my respects to all who may enquire after me.

Yours,
Will
Direct your letters to Washington City to be forwarded

On the 9th of November, the troops were at Warrenton, Virginia. "The whole army was massed in the vicinity of Warrenton and on the 10th the brigade went into camp and enjoyed a few days of rest as the weather and the roads along the mountain range had made the late march a laborious and uncomfortable one.

"It was officially known that McClellan had been relieved and command given to Gen. Burnside. He was given an enthusiastic welcome when he came to review the troops. On the 14th we moved toward Falmouth (VA). The 8th was very nearly in the same place as where it had burned Gen. King's new fence last spring.

"Temporary camps were established the next day, but supplies were limited and the weather was cold and inclement and the men suffered much. The baggage had been sent by way of Washington and not delivered.

"On the 18th the enemy appeared and the commanding officer went to examine the situation. They were on the opposite side of the Rappahannock in temporary rifle pits. The entire army was presently massed in this spot. Daily balloon reconnaissance was resorted to (the men expected Professor Lowe to go up along with his balloons)."

Sawyer's narrative states that the battle was scheduled to begin at 3 o'clock on the morning of the 10th of December. Some troops were massed behind a ridge in front of the Phillips mansion, some were near the Lacy mansion and something over 300 pieces of artillery were keeping up a constant bombardment of Fredericksburg. Bridges were laid as rapidly as possible even though the builders were harassed by rebel gunfire. A pontoon bridge was speedily laid and the first brigade went across.

"Gunners failed to get a ball or shell into our ranks although we were frequently spattered with mud. A most unearthly noise (something like the cross between a locomotive and a wild cat) was heard. The men and officers turned pale. The missile was a piece of rail-road rail with lead about the end, so as to fit a cannon. When it struck, it scooped out a big holes, and sent the mud over a whole brigade.

"We were forced to lie on the ground during the night with no protection but a blanket. The next morning, French's Division drew out and crossed on the pontoon bridge to the city. It had been pretty badly knocked about by our artillery and there was a great number of goods and debris on the ground. The men did not plunder except to replenish their tobacco pouches.

"The night was cold, dark and foggy. The rebels were completely obscured by the mists. We knew and felt the desperate character of the encounter before us.

"The 8th Regiment, the Fourth Ohio and First Delaware were assigned the duty of clearing the interval between the town and foot of the heights. The commanders job was to reconnoiter the ground around the town. A canal surrounds the city. The bridges were torn up and the canal itself was held by rebel sharp shooters. The town shops, homes, out buildings and gardens were held by a considerable detachment of troops. It was our job to drive these men back to their hillside.

"We got our forces into the city and were ready to move out. The column started at double-quick. As we came to the slight fall in the street as it approaches the canal, a terrible fire from the sharp shooters and several shells struck the head of the column. Over twenty officers and men fell. However, we were soon across. As soon as we rose over the little bank, missiles came upon us. Fences had to be pushed or cut down and several bogs caught the men in half a leg deep. The rebels gave way rapidly, not stopping to re-load, some surrendering after delivering their fire, as our men were now loading and firing as they moved.

"The fighting went on for several hours under withering fire. The plain in our rear now presented a most horrible sight. It was literally covered with dead and wounded. In one instance, some men were carrying a wounded man on a stretcher, when a shell exploding among them blew the whole party to atoms.

"As it began to grow dark, an order came to withdraw my command, which was done with but little loss. As we crossed the canal, we met a column of fresh troops, a division of Hooker's Corps moving to the front, but they were as unsuccessful as the others. The storm of battle raged for some time, gradually dying away and the troops were withdrawn to the city.

"Our brigade took up a position along the river bank and the men lay down to rest. We did not know why we did not continue the battle, but later learned that Gen. Burnside had been dissuaded from continuing the attack. Our forces continued to occupy the town until December 15, when we re-crossed the river and went back to our camp at Falmouth. Our losses were not as severe as at Antietam but it was nonetheless severe and caused a profound sense of sorrow. No other group was able to penetrate as close to the rebel lines as the 8th.

"We were ordered to build comfortable huts for the winter. Considerable changes had taken place by this time in the regiment. Several of the captains and lieutenants had resigned or been killed. Some four or five recruits arrived; but our recruiting officers reported that our reputation for getting into the front of all the hard battles did not commend the regiment to the favorable opinion of new recruits in Ohio."

The next letter from William F. Kimmell, Sgt., 8th Regiment O.V.I., was written from Romney, VA on December 20, 1862. There is no mention in this letter about the terrible battles he had just been in, only about Christmas and the winter camp.

My Dear Friend, Leah,

I received your kind letter a few days ago and haste to answer it for "I judge you by myself" you are always anxious for an answer.

I presume you are thinking of Christmas by this time and what good times you will have. My messmates are having a big argument this evening about who shall roast the goose for we are intent on having a goose for dinner, We can cook our own Christmas dinner and enjoy it, to. I had hoped to spend a few days at home about New Years, but I shall have to give it up. So you need not look for me until you see me.

We have had very pleasent weather for several weeks past, and I can hardly think it is as late in the winter as what it is. For I have always been used to seeing snow and very cold weather about Christmas. I wish you could see our camp as it looks at present. I will try and describe it the best I can. Each company has eighteen tents. They are set in rows about twenty feet apart, and nine in each row so that each company has its streets. There is a row of small evergreen trees on each side of the street. The officers tents are in one row back of the company with evergreens in front. And the camp is swept up as clean as any door yard. Our officers are very strict in regard to cleanliness and we have one of the best and finest appearing Regts in Romney.

I must drag this scribbling to a close. I sincearly hope you may enjoy your self during the hollidays and that I may yet ask the pleasure of accompanying you to a great many parties. I will now bid you Good Bye for a time.

Yours in Friendship,

W. F. Kimmell

Please direct your letters to Romney, VA

Letter to Kate Crispell written on the back of Leah's.

My Dear Friend,

I have a hard task before me trying to write and can't think of any thing to write. You may have been in the same fix and will know how to sympathise with me. I have been handling the musket so long that I can hardly do anything else. I am afraid that it will be a hard task for me if I ever go into society again. I couldn't converse on anything else but soldiering. But still I am in hopes that I will be able to learn again.

It is getting very late and I must quit. When you write again to E. Coates send him my best respects. I wish you all a Merry Christmas and now Friend, Kate, Good Bye for the present.
Will

—•—

Sawyer said that the weather was pretty severe; the supply of tents limited. The officer's baggage that had been sent from Harper's Ferry had not yet come up, and the Sutlers did not arrive with any goods until about the 15th of January. Much of the baggage was lost or stolen at Washington.

"There is something a little gloomy in the temper of the troops, and the entire camp atmosphere. We are somehow flooded with copperhead organs, boasting and blowing about their Butternut victory at the fall elections, denouncing Congress, cursing the President, sneering at the army and gloating over our recent defeat. Very little was said about our poor fellows who were almost constantly on duty in the cold, mud and rain. On the 17 of January Gen. Burnside reviewed the Second Corps and careful inquiries made and reports required as to our condition to take the field.

"The next day we were called on for heavy details of men to build roads, an immense "corduroy" being built back of the camp and leading to the fords on the river above our camp."

Will's next letter was from Camp near Falmouth, VA written on January 19, 1863

My Dear Friend,

Since I have heard from you that I am almost in dispair of ever hearing from you again. The last letter that I received from you was dated Nov. 18th. I answered it at the time and wrote another immediately after the Battle of Fredricsburg. I have no doubt but that you have the same thing to complain of. I know that if you have received my letters you have answered them and are waiting for me to write. I would write oftener than what I do if I were better situated for writing than what I am. There is five of us messing together in a little log hut 8 by 10 feet. It is always full. At this time there are six in besides myself, Three discussing the war, two playing checkers and one getting dinner. I never was much of a writer and when there is a noise and disturbance going on around me all the time, I can't write at all. There is nothing new going on here worth writing of. The rebels still lay on the opposite side of us as bold as ever. They have been throwing up fortifications ever since the battle. It was a strong position before, but it is almost impregnable now. We are under marching orders and we may leave in a few days and we may not go for a week or two. I don't think we will undertake to cross the river at this place. We will either go up or down the river. And its more than likely that we will not cross at all. Dinner is ready and I will bid you good bye for the present. I do hope this will bring me an answer.

My respects to all as usual,

W. F. Kimmell

—•—

Sawyer remarks that on January 20, Gen. French called out his division for drill, preparatory to do whatever we would be called on to do in eanest. General Bufford then moved up the river with a heavy column of cavalry The artillery was also moving sending masses of troops around the camp.

"But that evening," Sawyer said, "It began to rain, which for three days continued to fall in unremitting torrents. It was intended to throw a heavy force across the river at the fords above, to get in the rear of Lee's position, when the assault on Fredericksburg was again to be renewed by the Second Corps. The ground had become soaked to such a depth it was impossible to drag the artillery through it, and the infantry could not be moved over the spongy surface rapidly enough to ensure the success of the enterprise. It was therefore abandoned.

"Being in charge of the picket line along the river opposite Fredericksburg, we were soon aware of huge signs posted on the opposite side of the river by the rebel pickets, "Burnside is stuck in the mud."

"From the picket headquarters, at the Lacy House, their rejoicing in the city during the evening could be distinctly heard. Their bands were playing 'Dixie,' and the swell and chorus of song floated across to us in most taunting strains. Silence was required of our pickets, and they could not reply but we would have enjoyed answering with 'Yankee Doodle.'

The troops remained in winter quarters and heavy rains were constant for some weeks. The men, to relieve monotony of camp life had found some old fiddles, banjos and other instruments and with song and dance filled up the spare hours.

Burnside had resigned in February, and Gen . Hooker was appointed General in Chief. There was something in his manner and in his sobriquet of "Fighting Joe Hooker" that pleased the command. A visible new life and energy was imparted to the army.
William wrote to Leah on from camp. Sabbath Day

Feb. 15th, 1863

My Dear Friend,

I have received your most welcome letter just eleven days after it was written. It had been so long since I had seen your hand writing that I had almost forgotten it. I have to write.

Everything remains quite. It does nothing but rain all the time. The boys are all in bed, and have been putting in the time writing. Among others, I have written to Billy. Such long dreary days as these are ones that make me homesick.. What would I not give to spend a few days at home. It seems to me that we could spend a few hour together right plesantly. If we could not act over old times over again we could at least talk them over. It is not likely however that we are soon to have the pleasure of a personal interview. I do hope that the war may end before long. Yet I have no reason to complain. I have always had good health and have passed through so many battles unscathed. I rather have reason to be thankful. When I look around me and see what so many others have done and suffered in this cause, the common cause of humanity, I feel ashamed of not having done more myself. Yet I think that I have always done my duty when called upon. You cannot blame me if I sometimes speak despondingly of our prospects. A dark, dark cloud has settled over our future. I sometimes feel that all is lost and that torrents of blood have been spilt in vain. But than I look at our past history at the baptism of suffering and blood through which our Fathers passed. When I see and believe as I certainly do, that God has planted and fostered Constitutional Liberty here, I cannot think that he is now about to forsake us and suffer the last hope of oppressed humanity fo fail.

Let us hope yet though it may be in an unexpected way that our Government and institutions of Freedom will be preserved. And our Starry Banner once more float peacefuly and triumphantly over every state and Territory in this wide land.

I have noticed in the papers for some time that Indiana is forgetting her loyalty. It is the last state that I would have expected it from. Had it been Mass or some other abolition state I should not have wondered as much, but Indiana, never. The rebellion sympathisers are in the majority and are bound to rule. There ought to be a Regt of Union troops stationed in every county.

My respects as usual to all. I will close with my sincere wishes for your temporal and eternal welfare.

W. F. Kimmell
Co. C, 8th Regt OVI
Frenches Division
Falmouth, VA

General Hooker reviewed the troops on March 5 and the men had all been outfitted with new uniforms, belts, boxes and plates. The badge of each corps was of a particular design, which served to designate the divisions by the colors of red, white, and blue. The badge of the Second Corps was a trefoil, and that of the division, the Second, a white trefoil. Will wrote again to Leah on March 14, obviously quite homesick.

Camp Near Falmouth VA
March 14, 1863

Dear Leah,
Not more welcome is an inn to the sight of a weary traveller than was your kind letter to me. It was twelve days on the road. I don't know what the reason is that lately our letters are so long on the way. It used to take but four days for a letter, to come from Albion, here. The weather still continues bad. For the last two days it has been uncomfortably cold. I do wish the weather would settle so that we could make a move. This dull routine of camp life is almost killing me. There is nothing I do so hate as to be tied down to one thing day after day. I had much rather undergo the hardships of the march and I hate to be laying in camp stuck in the mud and get the papers every evening filled with the accounts of what our Armies are doing in the Southwest. I feel just as if we are not doing our share.

I have a year and one month yet to serve. I do hope that the war will end in that time for I never want to enlist again. Yet if I live to get through that time and the rebellion is not put down, I shall not hesitate long about enlisting again.

I have been in hopes of geting home a short time this spring but am afraid I shall be disapointed. You must please excuse me for not writing a very long letter. Their is times that I can't write at all, and at others I can write for hours withougt getting tired. This appears to be one of the former.

Sincerely yours,
W. F. Kimmell

————•—•————

"The 17th of March, St. Patrick's Day," Sawyer continued, "was observed by the brigade in true old fashioned Irish style. Gen. Meagher's Irish brigade was on the plain just above us, and the entire corps was considered as invited guests. The General was dressed in the character of "an Irish gentlemen of the ancient time." We had hurdle races, greased poles and greased pigs and enough fun to drive all the blues from the camp for any length of time.

"However the ceremonies were brought a sudden close when heavy firing was heard up the river and it was supposed that Averill had been attacked. Hearing no further commotion no march was designated."

Leah had written to Will on the 27th of March and had enclosed her miniature with it. He responded to her gift by letter written on April 3, 1863 from the camp near Falmouth, Va. across the river from Fredericksburg.

Dear Leah

Your welcome letter of March 27th I received this evening with much pleasure as your letters always are neither long or short The minature it contained made up more than you could have wrote. Please accept a thousand thanks for it. You have changed a great deal from what you were when your other miniature was taken and I think for the better. You look a great deal more womanly in this than what you do in the other.

I got a letter from your Brother William this evening dated March the 21st. He was well but complained of not hearing from home for five or six weeks. You ought to write to him often for I know how much he prizes letters from home. He is young and never from home until he went in the army and that is the very hardest school that a person can get into upon leaving home. I judge him by myself for I know how much I prize letters from home and I certainly have no perticular cause to do so. I don't think Billy is quite as Patriotic as he was before he inlistect. The wire edge is wore of at least Soldiering was not quite as easy as he expected to find it and he appeared to find it in its worst forms.

From the start he has good officers and that is one great consideration with a private soldier.

I am sorry that I was not permitted to spend a few days with my friends at home, but I have no reason to complain. There are several married men in our company that were not permited to go, and I think thay have more reason to complain than I.

We have one year from the 23rd of this month to serve and if it should be God's will to permit me to get safe through and restore peace to our once happy country, I will enjoy myself enough to make up for all privations that I am compelled to endure at the present time. Should this monster rebellion not be crushed in that time it may become my duty to enlist again, but it is of no use borrowing trouble for the future. We are in the hands of an over ruling Providence to be delt with as he sees fit, and let us hope for the best.

You spoke of going to Wolcotville to school this summer. I do wish that I could go to some good school for six months it would do me a vast deal of Benefit, and it is my intention to do so should I be spared through the war. I have had chances enough to become a good scholar but I never improved them.

I hope that your studies will not debar you altogether from writing to me, though I cannot expexct you to write as often as heretofore. Your letters have always been a source of much pleasure to me. You are the only one of my many correspondents that has always written cherring letters to me, for which I can never thank you to much. I shall close this scribling with my best wishes for your future welfare. Write at your first opertunity.

Yours in Sincerity
Wm. F. Kimmell

Sawyer said that the gloom which had been with the group since Fredericksburg was gradually disappearing and the espirit de corps of the army established. Governors of several states had visited, members of congress, fathers, brothers and friends of soldiers and on the 8th of April, the entire army was reviewed by President Lincoln. At daylight the artillery thundered a salute and the troops in review. Several ladies were present including Mrs. Lincoln with little Tad. The winter gave way to spring, the roads became passable and an advance on the enemy was being planned.

Colonel Samuel S. Carroll divison chief, reported in his official letter to Washington that had he been reinforced by troops at the battle of Chancellorsville, he would have defeated the enemy because he had them on the run. He described the gallant fight that the 8th Ohio put up in the woods and because other sections of his regiment were removed the 8th was left alone to defend its position. In spite of the fact that a retreat was necessary he did capture a small quanitity of ammunition, "1 major, 5 captains, 7 lieutenants and 270 enlisted men. I released a regiment of Zouaves belonging to the 3rd Corps who had been held prisoners behind the enemy rifle pits."

Sawyer describes the battle of Chancellorsville. "On the morning of the 2nd of May heavy artillery fire could be heard and the battle had begun for Chancellorsville. A group of fleeing men suddenly came up out of the dense woods in utter confusion. Orders were given to French's division to stop this 'tidal wave.' Gen. Hooker had withdrawn his troops from ground south of Chancellorsville and the turnpike and formed his line. This was his ground and Lee had elected to fight him on it."

The description from Sawyer's narrative tells of the loud and fierce fight. "The battle in our front now raged furiously, and as darkness came on the lurid glare from the batteries shone above the forest, the trail and exploding of shells lit up the heavens like fireworks. Our division did not move much from its position, but was kept in constant readiness for any emergency, fears being entertained that it was Lee's plan to seize the fords in our rear.

"The artillery firing continued until long into the night. The fact of a terrible defeat of our right wing was known to all. No one slept. Anxiety and excitement were everywhere."

Sawyer stated that although this was the scene of Stonewall Jackson's mortal wounding, the 2nd Corps was unaware of it. Intent on cutting off Hooker, Jackson went forward through the dark and tangled wood to inspect our position and on his return as he and his staff approached his own lines, he was mistakenly fired upon.

The next morning the 8th Regiment was ordered to a position near a farm-house and out-buildings, with directions to make temporary defences and to support a battery which was brought up and placed in the midst of the troops.

"Generals Hooker, Meade, Howard and other officers were soon on the spot. As J. E. B. Stuart's battle line developed, Col. Carroll, with three or four regiments of French's division attacked him furiously with the bayonet, driving his left flank across the pike road, and capturing a number of prisoners, but Stuart being reinforced, pressed French's line back and attacked at our right.

Sawyer continues."During this time our front had been to the west. The 8th was now ordered to form with its front towards Chancellorsville, in the neighborhood of which a battle was being fought. The Chancellor House had been shelled, set on fire, and was now burning to the ground.

"The situation was most precarious. We were in a dense oak swamp, through which shot and shell plunged everywhere. The road was choked up with mule teams, ambulances, artillery, officer and cavalry men plus a drove of cattle, horses without riders and confusion.

"The fight lasted several hours. The 8th was withdrawn and moved across open ground to rejoin our Brigade. The rebels were still shelling us. As we entered the woods in the rear of the plantation a shell exploded wounding three men of the eighth, and struck my horse, crippling him.

"The battle to most of us was a mystery. Believing at the outset that a great victory awaited us, we now found that the enemy had been whipped in detail, and now pushed back nearly to the river and yet at least two corps, Reynolds and Meade's had not been seriously engaged."

In Sawyers official report to Washington he commented on the bravery of his officers and men. His loss on Sunday was 7 wounded, and on Tuesday 1 private killed (Company D) and 3 wounded.

Will's letters continue with one written shortly after the engagements described above

Camp Near Falmouth, VA
May 8th, 1863

Dear Leah,

I will now attempt to answer your letter of April 19th. Since I last wrote you we have had another terrible battle with the enemy and have been defeated. I will not attempt to give you any of the perticulars of the engagement just now. We have just got back into our old camp today and consequently, everything is upside down, and out of order. I would not attempt to write at all were it not that we are very likely to move tomorrow and there is no telling when I might get a chance to write again.

For the first time during the war our Regt was not engaged in close action and I may be endebted to that lucky circumstance to be able to write this letter tonight. We were detailed as a support for artillery and did not get into close quarters with the enemy. Although we were exposed to artillery fire for three days by which we lost seventeen men

You must excuse me for not writing more this time. Should we stop in camp for a few days I will try and give you a more interesting of account of our trip across the river which did not turn out to be a very pleasent one I assure you. My thanks to Miss Foote for her compliments and my best wishes to her always. I hope that you may still enjoy your school life. Adieu for the present

Yours,
Wm F. Kimmell

Sawyer's account of life resumes by describing the time out from war which the 8th enjoyed at Fredericksburg. The group established a camp near the Warrenton Road where they had good springs and near plenty of water. The men had built comfortable houses, made neat streets, and shaded them with limbs and brush. The health of the troops was generally good and the sutlers stores were plenty. Plus they all had been paid. Hancock was frequently present at the drill and won the esteem of the men. The reconnaissance balloon was still going up and the 'aerial professor' quietly made telescopic observations of the rebel side until one day the rebels shot it down and the pickets reported that the rebels laughed and shouted with glee over its crashing. It was never used again.

Will's letter from Fredricksburg, VA written May 24, 1863 describes the time spent in camp.

Dear Friend,

Your letter of May 4th reached me yestarday. It was indeed welcome as all your letters are. You will see by this that we have joined Gen McDowells's army. (We are very likely to be in Richmond in the course of a week of so). We got here on Thursday last. Marching one hundred and fifteen miles in six days and a half.

We had a very hot and dusty time of it. We are now entirely out of sight of mountains, something that we have not been for ten months. This part of the country is not worth living in. Nothing but sand banks and pine ridges. There is some very elegant residences near Fredericksburg, but the town itself is a very poor looking place. Mrs. Washington, mother of Gen Washington, was buried here. A very fine marble column marks her last resting place

Yestarday for the first time we had one of the grand reviews for which the Potomac Army has been celebrated for a year past. President Lincoln was here. He complimented our division highly. I have no doubt but it was a splendid sight for the spectators to see 80,000 men maneuvering in the field. But for us who had to march around in the dust and heat for three hours it was anything but fine.

I have saw a number of old Albion acquaintances in the 19th Ind. Regt. They all appear to be in excellent spirits and anxious to have a hand in the victory. Our position in the army is in the first brigade of the first division. Gen Shields commands the division. Gen. Kimball the brigade. We will be in the advance. I thought I would tell you this so if you saw any accounts in the papers you would know what part we performed. I will close this scribbled letter hoping it may find you in as good health and spirits as it leaves me.
My kindest regards to Kate and all others. Your friend through life.

Will
Direct to Co. c 8th Ohio Regt
Shields Division
Washington, D. C.

＊━◆━＊

He wrote again to Leah on the 29th of May.

Camp Near Falmouth, VA
May 29th, 1863

Dear Leah,

It has been sometime since I have written to you and as I feel a little lonesome I know of no better way to pass the time than in writing again. I feel pretty certain that by this time, you are getting a little homesick and a letter now and then won't come amiss. I suppose by this time you have mastered all the hard points in your studies. I can imagine you this evening pouring over some hard lesson, just more than puzzling your brains to find the solution to it. And I can imagine your feelings after the lesson is mastered. I recollect what times I used to have, at the last school I attended. When I first went to work in Fort Wayne I attended an evening school. I had to work all day and poor chance to get my lessons. It used to trouble me a good deal and I know how good I used to feel when I would get the better of them.

I suppose you will think I am hard up for something to write about. I have written the first thing that came into my head, the thoughts of times past will come in to a persons head once in a while.

As to news concerning the army there is a dearth, everything is quiet. In my last I gave you a description of our trip across the river and the Battle of Chancellorsville. It would be useless to repeat it here. We will not be likely to move again very soon, unless the rebels force us to. This Army has been reduced to half its former size by the discharge of the two years and nine months men. I don't think the rebels will let us rest. now is the time for them to strike at this Army if they ever intend to.

I have not heard from your brother for some time. I suppose that he is with Grant's army at Vicksburg and is so busy that he doesn't get time to write.

I will close with an apology for the appearence of this letter. I have taken no pains with it. I need not ask you to write when you have an opportunity.

My respects to Miss Foote*, always, and accept my best wishes for yourself. Most sincerely yours,.

Wm. F. Kimmell

Kate married J. Calvin Foote

The army left its campgrounds and started moving upriver as they had heard reports of rebel movement toward them.

Sawyer said, "We moved slowly waiting for pickets to come up and arrived at Stafford Court House next morning. We had breakfast and resumed march . The day was intensely hot, the men suffered greatly and a great many were felled by heatstroke. That night we bivouacked near Acquia Creek and started march again at 3 in the morning. After a long march to Occoquan Creek, we halted for the night. The men were again suffering from the heat and lack of water. We made it to Fairfax Station on the Orange and Alexandria Railroad where we camped for three days. We heard all sorts of rumors about Lee. During the day the rebel scouts were hovering about us and the enemy was supposed to be by in great force. The next day, the 8th was thrown forward as a skirmish line toward Gainesville. We pushed carefully over a portion of the battle-field of Gainesville or second Bull Run. The sight we saw was most ghastly, as unburied skel-etons, bones and skulls lay scattered about the woods; sometimes half-buried remains extend their skeleton hands imploringly toward us."

From then until the 27th of June the troops were kept busy marching. It had been raining constantly and all of the previous marching men had ground the land into a quagmire. The whole army of the Potomac were in the vicinity. On the 30th of June they were in Uniontown, Pennsyl-vania.

Sawyer continues," The advance of our army was now beyond Gettysburg, and heavy fighting reported. We broke up camp in the forenoon and marched towards Gettysburg, the roars of artillery indicating a severe battle in that direction."

Soon after this march the 8th met General Hancock who told them that he had selected a position from which Lee could not drive them and there the battle would be fought.

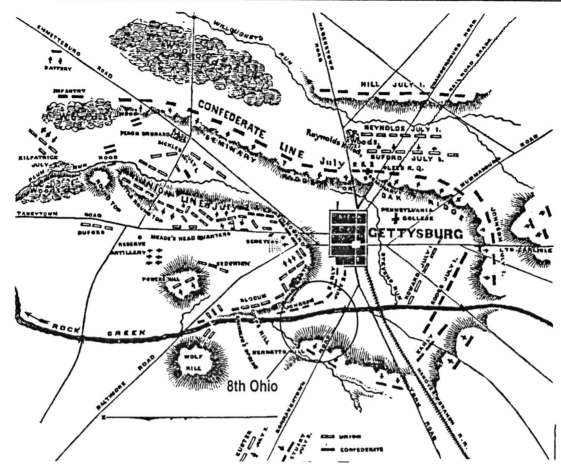

"We lay on our arms during the night, some two or three miles from Gettysburg, and were aroused and in motion before daylight. We moved up near the front and halted near various armies while the men refurbished their arms, getting cap and cartridge boxes in shape and preparing for the fight that all knew to be immediately before us.

"Gen. Hooker had been recently relieved and the army was now in command of Gen. Geo. G. Meade. This change of commanders hardly elicited a comment. The battle was their paramount theme."

On the 2nd of July the entire army was at Gettysburg with the exception of Sedgwick's corps.

"Our division, the 2nd., formed near Howard fronting the Emmettsburg Road. The formation of the line at this point resembled the letter U. Nearly in the center of the position occupied by our division, was Seminary Ridge. It was comparatively quiet for several hours, but within our lines there was activity. Large detachments of troops were in motion, artillery being got into position, ammunition trains, caissons and limbers pounding about over the roads, the gloomy ambulances rattling along with their moaning occupants. Still our tired men gladly snatched even this interval for a little rest.

Col Carroll ordered the Eighth to be in readiness to make a sortie upon a ridge behind the Emmettsburg Road where the enemy were in a natural rifle pit and shooting 'whizzing minies' among the men. The area that they would cover was six hundred yards and mostly a 'red top' meadow. Sawyer jumped his horse over a stone wall and ordered the men to follow him. "The balls came thick and spitefully among us, the men began to fall, some killed, some wounded, but on we swept until we came to the fence along the Emmettsburg Road, from which the rebels retreated in great haste."

"We took the next fence and we were hand to hand with the rebels. Some 60 or 70 surrendered, but most of them hurriedly retreated. Thirteen men had been wounded and one killed and my horse had been struck several times and was sent to the rear."

The struggle between Sickle's Corps and Longstreet was visible to the men. They knew from the battle that the whole front would soon be involved. Two companies were sent forward and the balance of the regiment was ready to attack. Several more were wounded.

"Then a terrific cannonade burst forth beyond Cemetery Hill. Balls from the rebel batteries burst down on us and I sent back to Col. Carroll to tell him our our position. No reinforcements were sent to us as all were employed. We, however, suffered no further attack in force during the evening but were constantly harassed by sharp-shooters." The rebel forces attacked the early morning and were repulsed by the 8th.

Sawyer's tale continues, "On the morning of July 3 a terrific cannonade opened up and about 150 rebels formed a semi-circle around our position. This fire was replied to by an equal number of our guns. Nothing more terrific than this storm of artillery can be imagined. The missiles of both armies passed over our heads. The roar of the guns was deafening, the air was soon clouded with smoke, and the shriek and startling crack of exploding shells, the blowing up of our caissons in the rear, the driving through the air of fence-rails, posts and limbs of trees; the groans of dying men, the neighing of frantic and wounded horses, created a scene of absolute horror. We sat down in a cut of the road for nearly two hours and not a word was uttered. Only two or our men were killed during the cannonade, and they were literally cut in two.

"We knew that something would soon happen. We saw the long line of rebel infantry emerge from the woods that hitherto concealed them. These troops were the division of Pickett, followed by that of Pettigrew. They appeared not to see us, but then a strong line directed its march immediately upon us.

"I directed our men to shoot. We charged them. Some fell, some ran back, most of them, however, threw down their arms and were made prisoners. The front of the rebel column was nearly up the slope when suddenly a terrific fire from every available gun, from the Cemetery to Round Top Mountain, burst upon them. The distinct, graceful lines of the rebels underwent an instantaneous transformation.

"They were at once enveloped in a dense cloud of smoke and dust. Arms, heads, blankets, guns and knapsacks were thrown and tossed into the clear air. Still the column advanced amid the now deafening roar of artillery and storm of battle.

"Suddenly, the column gave way, the sloping landscape appeared covered, all at once, with the scattered and retreating foe. A withering sheet of missiles swept after them. It seemed as if not one could escape. Of the mounted officers who rode so grandly in the advance not one was to be seen on the field, all had gone down.

"The Eighth advanced and cut off three regiments or remnants of regiments, as they passed us, taking their colors, and capturing many prisoners

"The battle was now over. The field was covered with the slain and wounded, and everywhere were to be seen white handkerchiefs held up asking for quarter. The rebel loss had been terrible, the victory to the Union army complete.

"The Eighth, when we received the order to take this position, numbered present for duty, 209 officers and men, of these 102 were killed and wounded. We were relieved soon after battle, and with the little remnant of the regiment, we marched back to within our lines. For nearly two days our little band had stood alone nearly a half mile in advance of the battle line.

"On the morning of the fourth of July, we collected and buried our dead near a walnut tree in the vicinity of a farm house, marked their graves and built a rail fence around them. No duties were required of us during the 4th of July, and the men for the greater part of the day remained quietly in their shelter tents, and sought the rest so much needed . On the 5th, we moved out about two miles, fording a swollen creek, and bivouacked in an open wood."

Camp Near Gettysburg, PA
July 6th 1863

Dear Leah,

It has been sometime since I have written to you. It has not been through neglect that I have not done so. We have been on the move for some time and opportunities to write have been rare. But it useless my saying anything to you of it because I know you would excuse me were I not to write for three months under present circumstances. When this reaches you I expect you will be enjoying yourself at home. I had made big calculations on spending the 4th of July at home. But I certainly have reason to be thankful that I did not spend it laying cold in death on the bloody field of Gettysburg. Two more of my companions have given up their lives to the cause of our country, and seven have been wounded. There is but eleven of us left out of the ninety-eight that came into Virginia two years ago. My chances are growing smaller all the time. One more hard battle and there will be no more Co. C.

I wish I were able to describe the Battle of Gettysburg. It is not worth while to try it, for I should fail. If you can get the New York Herald, you will find as good an account as is possible to give. They have one of the best of correspondents with this army.

People say that a person gets hardened by seeing suffering. It is just the reverse with me. I am getting so that I can hardly bear the sight of a wound. I never want to look over a battle field after a battle. I see citizens here that have come over a hundred miles to see the field, and appear to be greatly disappointed because the dead are most all buried before they got to see them. I must say though that the wounded never were as well taken care of as they are here. The citizens pour in from all directions with delicacies and comforts for the wounded. I will have to close my letter as it is not a very comfortable position setting with my back against a fence corner, and a stave of barrel on my knee for a desk. Always give my respects to all enquiring friends and write as often as possible.

My Best wishes are always yours,
Wm. F. Kimmell

Direct to Washington, D.C.
I send you a relick of the Battlefield

—•—

Colonel Sawyer continues his narrative by telling that after the battle the troops remained in the area for several days recuperating. He also went out into the area visiting farmhouses dickering for food. One woman he described as being a lineal descendant of some original Hessians because she spoke bad English, bad French but good Dutch. "She refused to let them in her kitchen saying that they were too ornery. She wanted a dollar for a gallon of milk and half dollar for a cruet of vinegar," Sawyer refused to pay her prices but he noted that his cook was not inclined to argue the point and at the next meal the troops were served chicken for breakfast.

After resting for several days and finally securing fresh rations and most of all getting new shoes the troops remained in the area of Warrenton, VA and received their pay. On August 15, the 8th and 4th Ohio, the 14th Indiana and some 1800 other troops were order to proceed to Alexandria by rail and then by steamer to New York City, where they were to quell the riots and protect the draft in the city. As Sawyer said the men were unspeakable happy over this order and he never saw troops move more swiftly to obey. They sailed aboard the steamer Atlantic with their horses, knapsacks, guns and provisions. The weather, for once, was perfect. Most of the men had never seen the ocean so the decks of the ship were crowded with men watching. The accomodations were excellent and only a few of them became seasick. (The opposite of Will's opinion.)

On the 23rd of August they were off Sandy Hook and running down the Narrows. They anchored off Governor's Island and went into camp south of the fort. Here Will's letter to Leah is dated on August 25, 1863

Governor's Island, NY
August 25th, 1863

Dear Leah,

After this longest delay, I will again attempt to write you a letter. Since I last wrote you we have traveled over several hundred miles of land and sea.

We left the banks of the Rappahanock river on the 15th of this month. We came by rail to Alexandria, VA. We were there embarked on the steamship Atlantic for this place. We were on the water forty eight hours. Twenty four of which we were out of sight of land. There was considerable sea sickness on board but I was fortunate enough to escape it.

We are camped in one of the most delightful spots in the vicinity of New York City.

Governors Island contains about forty acres. Ft. Columbus is on this island. There is also a military hosptial, arsenal and grave yard. There are soldiers buried here that were killed in the Revolutionary war and also some that were killed in every war since then.

It is about a half mile to Brooklyn and one Mile to New York City.

I have been to the city twice and have been running around all the time. And have hardly seen one corner of the city yet. I have seen a great deal of the United States since I have been soldiering. I have been in six different states. Two of which I have been over on foot with a knapsack on my back. Big Maryland and Virginia.

I am in hopes we will be left here for the rest of our time for I have seen as much hard service as I wish to see.

I will close this dull letter with a promise to write again in a few days. Should anything occur worth writing. My respects to all as usual. My best wishes are always yours.

Adieu for the present.
Yours,
Wm. J. Kimmell
Direct , Co C, 8th Regt, Ohio Vol
Governors island
New York Harbor

———•———

Sawyer says that they had a great time for a few days. There were no duties and the riot squelched itself when the citizens of New York saw the blue coats. Many visitors from the city and many Ohio friends visited the troops at the camp. They had much fruit, which was a rarity in battle conditions, and the owners of the "Evening Post" sent each member of the regiment a daily paper. They were entertained by church people and other organizations. Most of this was over-whelming to the men who had seen nothing but camp life for over two years and the efforts of the citizens were most appreciated by the soldier. The men visited the city, attended church on Sun-day, saw the sights and were happy.

The draft continued safely and the "Copperhead" and the rebel subsided. The campaign to New York was complete and orders came to strike the camp and proceed to the Potomac.

Sawyer remarked that, "On the afternoon of September 7th we left 'Camp Green' Long Island and were landed by ferry boats at the foot of Wall Street, marched thence to Broadway, up Broadway to Canal Street, down Canal Street to North River and conveyed to our steamer. Along the whole line of march we were greeted by the waving of flags, of handkerchiefs by the ladies, and cheers from the crowd that lined the streets." The next morning they weighed anchor and returned to Alexandria on the 10th of September. They were proud of their country, pleased to have had a chance to see New York and were thrilled to have been entertained so royally by the citizens of New York. Saywer said that the men felt more patriotic, more willing and ready than ever to fight for the cause and the flag.

Unfortunately for Will his desire to not see any more service was not to be as the 2nd regi-ment camped near the Culpepper Court House , Virginia, was waiting their arrival to begin the campaign again. The corps was now commanded by General Warren. Sawyer said that Lee had learned that the Army of the Potomac had been somewhat depleted and picked this occasion to begin a battle. So the 2nd Corps moved forward to the Rapidan River where the rebels had set up their battle positions. They spent several days fighting little skirmishes. The most serious diversion happened when the division was called out to witness the first military execution that had occured in the corps. Two privates from the 14th Connecticut were shot for desertion, "bounty jumping" and conspiracy with outside villains and sharpers.

The 8th spent 4 days picketed along the Robinsons River near the junction with the Rapidan. The troops managed to acquire spoils from the retreating rebel forces, forage, cattle, mules and some saddle horses. After several marches the 8th returned to Bealton Station after having been marching and countermarching for two days and one night with little time for sleep or rest. They expected to have breakfast at this spot when they were ordered to support some cavalry under the command of General Custer. This was the 15th day of September and was election day for Ohio.

In the midst of the skirmish the men took time out to vote, arranging the polls "according to law." Sawyer says that the men voted quietly without speeches, harangues, or challenging, casting one hundred and ninety votes for John Brough for Governor, and one for Vallandingham, every voter present depositing a ballot.

Sept 24th, 1863

Dear Leah,

Again will I attempt to write you. We have changed our base of operations since I last wrote you. We have taken our old place in the Army of the Potomac. At the present writing we are bivouacked in the woods near the Rapidan River. We have been expecting to have a battle every day—but—the Rebs are a little shy and are trying to avoid a battle. If Meade makes another advance we will most certainly have a collusion. If they intend to fight us at all it will be between here and Gordonsville and we are now only fifteen miles from that place. I would rather prefer to have no battle at all, for I only have seven months from today to serve as a soldier. I've no desire at all to have an ounce of lead put in me at this late day. There was once a day that I was anxious for a battle but I have got over that. I have seen battles enough to last me a life time. I do sincerely hope the war may be ended during my term of service. I never want to re-enlist. Still I shall be glad to get home and return to civil when my time is out, but how much greater would that enjoyment be, should the rebellion be crushed and we would all be able to return to our homes to peace and quiet. Won't that be a proud day to us when it is proclaimed through the land the rebellion is crushed and the "cruel war is over?" May that day soon come is my earnest wish.

One of our greatest victories will be defeating the traitor Vallandingham* for Governor of Ohio. We have a chance of voting at the coming election and you can be assured their will be no votes cast by the Ohio soldiers in this army for Vallandingham. I will bring my letter to a close as I can think of nothing worth writing. Should you see any of my folks tell them where I am. I don't get opportunities for writing home as often as I would like. Remember me to Kate, and all other friends who may enquire of me.

Yours truly,
Wm. J. Kimmell
Direct as usual

* Clement Vallandigham was an Ohio politician who criticized President Lincoln's war policies. He favored compromise with the south and was arrested and charged with treason in 1863. He was banished to the Confederacy by the president, but he escaped to Canada. During his exile he was nominated for governor, but he lost the election. He returned to the U. S. in 1864, but he never regained political power.

Between the time that the voting took place and Will wrote his next letter the 8th underwent more fighting along the Rappahannock River. They were in severe fights with Hill's army and with Lee's. They crossed and recrossed the river, they captured many horses, wagons and provisions as well as 600 prisoners. They also retreated, but eventually their superior forces prevailed and Lee retreated. On the 19th of October they struck their tents and moved back again toward the Rappahannock . As Lee retreated he destroyed the railroads and bridges. They camped that night at Bristoe Station and marched the next morning toward Warrenton and forded the Broad Run no less than three times during the day. They camped at this site (Auburn) for 9 days when they finally moved to Warrenton. All of this William F. described by saying that Leah would read accounts of this in the paper

Oct 20th 1863

Dear Leah,

I received your letter this evening and answer immediately. Although my facilities for writing are very poor. We have been marching all day and I am writing this by a fire at nine o 'clock at night. I can't see the lines more than half the time but I guess you can make it out. We only have a mail once a week and it goes out in the morning so I write now. We have been marching day and night for the past week and have fought one severe battle, Bristoe Station. You no doubt have had full accounts of it. Our Corps, the 2nd done its duty. Our Regt did not suffer very severely as we fought behind shelter. We had three men wounded severly as all the casualties. We are thankful it was no worse. We held our election while the Rebels were shelling us. One hundred and ninety one votes were cast for Brough and one for Vallandingham. That vote was cast in my company though you can be assured it was not cast by me.

Nothing pleases us more than the results of the recent elections in the north. It will help end the war more than a hundred thousand men.

The President's Proclamation calling for three hundred thousand men to take our places is another move in the right direction. I want to see every available man in the north brought into the field. One man is no better than another in his country The success of our cause will benefit all and why not all help to achieve that result.

They are trying to re-enlist all the old troops. Many are joining for three years longer. I will never re-enlist until I get clear of this term. I have other objects in view and I think three years of constant service is my share. Yet there is no telling what the next year will bring forth. Man proposes and God disposes.

I will close by asking you to excuse my writing. Consider the circumstances in which it is wrote. I feel like writing and could write all night but we march at daylight and I must get some rest. Please write soon and direct as before though it is more certain to put on the division and company 8 and second.

Good-bye. Hope you may sleep sound tonight as I shall if I am not disturbed.

Yours as ever,
Wm. F. Kimmell

While camped at Warrenton Will received a letter from Leah and wrote to her about his feelings of the war and the loss of his comrades. In it he mentions his tent mate, M. Blanchard, who had been wounded but was once again with the company. WF was to name his oldest son, William Blanchard Kimmell.

Camp 8th Ohio Regt.
Near Warrenton, VA
Nov 4th, 1863

Dear Leah,

This evening I was again the happy recipient of another of your ever welcome letters. I don't know as I shall ever be able to repay you for the pleasure I always derive from your excellent letters. What a great difference there is in the tone of your letters and some I occasionally receive. Your are always cheerful, never finding fault, never complaining. You are a true friend of the soldier. At present I can do no more than to again repeat my thanks. At some future day it may be possible that I can do more than repeat my thanks but war is so uncertain, and the future is in the hands of a higher power than mine.

As an instance of the uncertainty of war I will relate a little of the history of our company. When we came into Virginia two years ago last July, we were given what is called tent to contain six men each. In the tent with me were six healthy young men, W. N. Williams. M. Blanchard, B. J. Monroe, J. K. Barkley, L. G. Snowden and myself. We made an agreement to stick to one another through the war. How far we have done so you will see. We passed through the various skirmishes up to the battle of Winchester all safe. We all came out safe with the exception of a slight wound on myself. We had the same good fortune through all the various skirmishes in the Shenandoah Valley up to the Battle of Antietam. There my best friend and comrade, L. G. Snowden, was instantly killed. Shot through the heart with a minie ' ball. Poor fellow, he never knew what hurt him. We buried him where he fell, but he has since been taken up and laid beside his parents in Pennsylvania. Williams and Monroe were both severely wounded and did not join the company again until after the battle of Fredericksberg.

Fredericksburg and Chancellorsville we came through safe. But on the bloody field of Gettysburg two were laid in soldiers graves. Williams and Barkley, the later the only son of a widowed mother. Monroe was severely wounded and will never do duty in the company again. Blanchard was also slightly wounded but is again with the company.

Today we were fixing up the tent when it came across my mind where are now those six who helped fix up the tent two years ago. Three have delivered up their lives on the altar of their country, while the fourth is a hopeless cripple. Two are left, but will any be left to tell the tale when the war is over. None know but God.

This is a true but sad story that I have written. My comrade and I had just been talking it over as we sat in the little tent this evening when your letter was handed to me. I sat down to reply. It was the first thing that came into my head. And I have written it. We have had a pleasent Indian summer for the past few days but tonight it looks like a storm. We will be very apt to move from here in a few days. When or which day we will go I have no idea. There is a thousand one rumors flying about camp as to where we will go. Some have us going to Tennessee. Some back to Washington to winter and some have us going toward Richmond. I don't trouble myself about it. When we get to our destination we will know all about it. I have scribbled over a good deal of paper and the bugle has just sounded lights out. So I will turn into my couch of down and dream of the good times I am going to have when I get to be a free man once again.

Adieu dear friend for the present.

Yours,

Will

Sawyer's story continues, "We remained in this camp until the morning of November 7, when a general forward movement was made. We moved to Kelley's Ford, being joined there by the First Corps commanded by Gen. Newton. The 2nd and Third Corps deployed at Kelly's Ford, throwing forward strong lines of skirmishers and sharp shooters. Batteries were planted on the range of hills, sweeping the position of the rebels on the south side of the river, under cover of which the pontoons were laid, and a heavy force was thrown across which charged the rifle pits, capturing several hundred prisoners. Our loss did not exceed seventy. General Sedgwick crossed the river at Rappahannock Station, stormed the rebel works, capured four guns, eight battle flags and nearly 2,000 prisoners, including numerous officers.

"The second and Third Corps moved rapidly forward to Brandy Station, the advance skirmishing most of the way. The rebel army retreated rapidly toward the Rapidan. On the morning of the 10th, we went into camp on the Hamilton Plantation. There was some little snow on the ground, and the tops of the mountains west of us were white. Our camp soon moved to a pine wood where we remained until the morning of the 26th of November—Thanksgiving Day—when the whole army was again put into motion."

The next major battle was Mine Run. The Second Corps, under command of General Warren, crossed the river at Germania Ford on a pontoon. They marched six miles and bivouacked in the forest. Then the next morning they went onto the Orange Court House Road. The 8th Regiment was sent forward as skirmishers toward a ridge of mountains which overlooked the enemy's advanced line. They had some cavalry with them in the front which shot at the enemy. The 8th was ordered to advance through the woods and drive out whatever they might find in the front. The 14th Indiana and the seventh Virginia were to move down the road and over an open plantation to their left.

Sawyer reports "For some unexplained reason, when the 8th moved forward, Gen. Webb's line at our right, remained stationary, thus leaving a gap which the rebels were not slow to discover and take advantage of. Capts. Pierce and Reid were in reserve, and as soon as the eruption of rebels on our flank and right rear was discovered, Reid wheeled his company the the right flank, confronted the rebels and a brisk skirmish ensued. Our right was doubled back and for a moment thrown into confusion. Capt Pierce brought his company up, and Gen. Webb now moving forward, our line was again formed and ordered forward to the line of a plantation in front.

"The rebels were keeping up a sharp fire and just as they cleared the thick woods a volley from a nest of Negro huts tore through the trees around us. I wheeled my horse to the right to gain some cover, when a ball, cutting through the stirrup strap and grazing my leg, went literally through 'Old Sam' and down we went together, the horse being instantly killed."

Sawyer said that the rebels were driven away and the line halted on the margin of the woods. Two men were killed from the 8th regiment. The 14th Indiana lost one killed and several wounded and in the 7th Virginia one person was wounded.

They maintained their position until 10 o'clock at night when they withdrew behind the battle line. The next day they spent shivering around the camp fires in a cold, drenching rain which then turned to snow. They joined up with the 4th Ohio and 14th Indiana and picketed the Corps during the long, stormy night.

On the morning of the 29th of November the 8th made a long a long slow march through the tangled underbush. They came upon the enemy in the afternoon and a brisk fight ensued. Then the enemy retired beyond Mine Run and the corps went into bivouac in a cold snow storm without tents for shelter. The troops expected a great battle to be fought the next morning and were aware of their desperate situation. The men were aroused at four in the morning and the battle line formed at six. They were to simultaneously advance with all the other troops. The Regiment had seen the long line of heavy earth and log works, battle flags, mounted batteries, bristling bayonets, and had heard cheering and shouting in reponse to the enemy generals orders. As the morning approached the troops formed into three lines. Each regimental commander examined the area in his front. Sawyer said he advanced to within pistol shot of the enemy.

All were aware of their perilous situation. The area was heavily fortified and a marshy strip of ground was between the Union forces and the river. The opposite banks of the river were almost perpendicular and crowned with strong works. The turnings of the stream made splendid positions for gunfire.

The men were most anxious—aware of the danger before them but not fearful. They all knew, as Sawyer exclaimed, that a terrible conflict must ensue in trying to carry the enemy's position, and but few could escape. Some of the men had written personal statements telling of their apprehension about the coming battle. These were pinned to their shirts along with their names and addresses.

The advance was to have begun at 8, but no order was given. They stacked their guns and kindled fires as the day wore on. At nightfall the men were directed to build fires, cook their supper and make themselves comfortable. Then at nine o'clock they were ordered to quietly fall in; the fires were replenished, and they drew out silently, and with the head of the columns turned and marched back towards the Rapidan. The army had been cut loose from its trains and supplies, with eight days' rations; winter was closing in and further operations were deemed impractical.

General Meade's plan for this campaign are said to have been elaborate and of a high military character, but an endless variety of circumstances had retarded his movements, and when the morning of the 30th came, he found that Lee's position was impregnable. It is said that General Warren took the responsibility of not ordering the attack. His judgement has been sustained.

During the night, the entire army withdrew, and on the morning of the 2nd of December they re-crossed the Rapidan and by nightfall were back in quarters. Sawyer said they were tired and disappointed because they had no glorious achievements to write of in their letters. The Regiment moved three times before they set up their comfortable winter quarters. The time was spent in picket duty and in building corduroy roads for the balance of the cold and stormy month.

Will's next letter to Leah was written on December 4.

Camp 8th Ohio Vol.
Dec 4th 1863

Dear Leah,

We got mail today, the first for seven days. In it were five letters for me, among them yours. I assure you it was the first one opened. I was delighted with its sentiments. They are mine exactly. You wonder who it is that writes complaining letters to me. They come principally from Ohio friends. I traveled over the country a great deal for several years before I came into the service and as a consequence picked up a good many friends that I have to maintain correspondence with. Though I can assure you it was not Elsie that wrote any of them. I have not wrote nor received a letter from her for over a year and as she has married. I never expect to.

We have just returned from a weeks trip toward Richmond. We had no general engagement though we were constantly skirmishing with the enemy. Our little company lost two men. I don't know what the object was in crossing the river and again falling back without a battle unless it was to create a diversion in favor of Burnside. We have been ordered to build winter quarters and I don't think we will have anything more to do this winter unless the rebels advance on us.

In my last letter I think I gave you a history of six comrades in this company, In this I have to add one more to the list of those that are gone. In the skirmish on the 27th of November, Sgt. Blanchard was severly wounded in the right elbow. So severely as to make amputation necessary. I parted with him today. I am now the last one of the six left in the company. I have written to the friends of the five that have gone before me. Who will write to my friends should anything befall me? And who will write the history of those six? Why should they all go before me?. I was always considered the smallest and the weakest one of the lot.

"Truly the ways of Providence are strange."

Leah, I think that I've never told you that I have lost your miniature but it is so. I had quite a collection of miniatures and trinkets and theyall were lost in our trip to New York. They were with the company things and were loaded and unloaded so often that they were mislaid. It was a course of great annoyance to me as I had things that I taken a great deal of pains to preserve. Before many months I expect to be able to see the originals of my miniatures so it is no use mourning the shadow. I will close for want of a fitting subject to write. I might write over several sheets and then not get anything in it that would interest you. My letters generally have one good point about them. If they are dry it don't last long . My respects to friends always. And for you permit me a verse.

May thy life be happy, Leah
Placid as the summer sea
Like the quiet evening hour
May thy thoughts as peaceful be.

And as time goes gently on
May no sorrows shade thy brow
But each hour be fraught with bliss
Bright and joyous e'en as now.

And when life is ended here
May thou gently sink to rest
Sweetly pass away from earth
Leaning on the Saviour's breast.

Will

⟨divider⟩

WF received a letter from Leah on the 13th of December and feeling quite homesick he wrote to her on the 19th as the regiment was preparing its winter quarters. He expressed his opinion on the worth of the southern forces and the invincibilty of the Union army. He also stated to her of his wish that he had a chance to go to school. The letter is datelined Stevensburg, VA.

Camp Near Stevensburg
December 19th, 1863

Dear Leah,

I hasten to acknowledge the reception of your very welcome letter of the 13th inst. I answer immediately because tis said that "Procrastination is the thief of time." and not because of a great quantity of news that I may have to write. The movements of this army are over for the present and will not be again resumed untill the balmy days of Merry springtime come again with its zephyr breezes scattering sweet incense over the face of all nature and—God dries up this horrible Virginia mud. Then and not till then will the Army of the Potomac again take up its march "On to Richmond." We lose nothing just now by remaining idle. While the Rebel time is everything. With the loyal Armies of the United States filled up with what men have been recently called out, they will be invincible. Another winter's starvation to the rebels and one or two good substantial victories in the spring will close up this unholy rebellion. Already do we hear wailing from their Chief Magistrate, Jefferson Davis, and not only from him but from throughout the whole South.

May the day soon come when the rebels will lay down their arms and sue for protection under the old starry banner and peace and plenty again reign triumphant through out our beloved land. And all such soldiers as myself be permitted to return to our peaceful homes and get married. "Law Sakes" won't that be fine.

I don't see why you should dread going to school. I am sure there is nothing I would like better than to go to some good school three months just now.

I have some pleasent recollections of my former school days in Albion among others that of a certain young lady, who then wore short dresses and now I presume is one of the belles of Albion society. Carrying around a tale about a certain young man still living in Albion, and myself being the two worst boys in school. Quite a compliment to us.

You are perfectly excusable for the mistake in speaking of Elsie as there was no harm done. And for the benefit of the Misses Haney, I will say that I am in regular correspondence with no less than five different young ladies and will write as many more as will write to me, and lest they should have curiosity to know more, I will say that I am engaged to none, and am not going to be until I quit being a soldier, whatever my feelings may be now, I am a soldier and use a soldiers priviledges and I would advise certain persons not to be so critical.

You are at perfect liberty to show this letter to those persons. if you wish to. I'd rather you would than not.

I suppose by the time this reaches you, you will have received a Christmas present from me in the shape of a book. It was to have been sent from New York about the 12th inst. It was purchased for me by a female friend residing there. A sister of my captain.

I will close with respects to friends

Ever your friend
Wm. F. Kimmell

Sawyer reports that the troops were provided with turkey, chicken and generous supplies for the holidays from friends, aid societies and the holiday was generally a good one. During the entire month of January, the duties of the men were the usual routine of picketing, fatigue parties, building roads, and occasionally regimental, brigade and division drill. During this time Will wrote twice to Leah describing camp life and thanking her for writing. The second letter he puts forth his feelings about home news and gossip.

Camp 8th Ohio Vol Infantry
Near Brandy Station, VA
Jan 7 1864

Dear Leah,

It is with pleasure that I again acknowledge the receipt of your welcome letter of a recent date. I would have a long dull evening hanging on my hands were it not for the pleasure of writing to you. I have been playing cook today and it would have done you good to have stepped into our hut this aftenoon. And seen me with my sleeves above elbows and all over flour, sweating over the fire.

You would have scarcely credited reports of sodiers hardships. Well I guess you are wondering all this time what I've been cooking. Well in the first place I cooked eighteen large apple dumplings for dinner and as there was only four us to eat them and we only left two of them, you can judge whether they were good or not and this afternoon I baked thirteen dried apple pies. Now is not that doing tolerable well considering that I had nothing but a dutch oven to bake them in, and for supper we had mashed potatos, fried beef, bread butter and tea. You will think we are living very well, and in truth we are, but it is not always so. We are like the Indians when we have it we live well, and then starve several days untill we get more.

I am really glad to hear that you are pleased with your Chrismas present. I had intended to send you an Album, but supposed that a suitable book would be more acceptable.

Be kind enough to return my compliments to Miss Aby and H. Haney. I should like to have them drop me a line. I need not remind them that this is Leap Year. I am afraid that this is not going to be a very interesting letter so the quicker it is closed the better. If it pleases you to write again tell me more about your school. Does the New School house stand in the same place the old one did? Write all about it. My thanks for your good wishes. I shall pass a happier year of 1864, especialy the latter part of it, than I have for the past two.

My respects to all my old school mates. With apologies for the briefness of this I will close,.

I remain always your friend
Wm. F. Kimmell

Camp 8th Ohio Vol
January 24, 1864

Dear Leah,

I must again thank you for your excellent letter and your promptness in writing. You certainly do not think that I do not wish you to write me, but pschaw, there is no use saying anything further about it. You cannot think me as great a hypocrite as that. I have received some letters from home, or rather from Albion, asking me if there was nothing more than mere friendship in our correspondence. Now their gossip does not trouble me in the least, but with you it is different, your are among them and hear it every day. I have often thought of writing to you on this subject, but as it is rather a delicate subject, I have not done it. How the rumor could have started, that we stood in nearer relation to one another, than mere friends, I am at loss to understand. I certainly never wrote or said anything that could have led to it. But it is not me, but you, that it affects.

I have always written to you as a friend, and have never implied anything further. A woman does have the same priveledge as a man in regards to matrimonial affairs, and I would wish to stand in the way of no one. I would wish no lady to lose an opportunity on my account.

You may think it strange in me writing in this way but I think we will both feel better for understanding one another. I have always treated you with perfect confidence and honor, more so than I ever did any other person; and shall always continue to do so. If I have any different feelings towards you than that of a friend, this would hardly be the time or place to tell of it. I will say no more on this *subject while I am a soldier, but when I get to be a free man again (which will be just three months from today) I can then speak more free. I trust that I 've said nothing out of the way in this or anything that will give offence, if so, I beg pardon.*

I am glad to know that my old school mates think of me sometimes. May they never have cause to change their opinion of me. I've always been fortunate enough to make friends wherever I went, and in no place more so than in the army. I don't know why it is, I am usualy called a wild boy, and I am in one sense of the word, as big a devil (excuse the expression) as any of them; I wrote to Cale McMeans today. He is my most particular friend. I don't suppose the letter you read proved very interesting. I hardly ever write a letter that is readable to a second person. In fact some I wrote won't stand reading by another person, this one for instance. Your wonder if it won't seem nice when I get to be a free man again. To use a camp expression, you can bet some on that.

Has Billy reinlisted again. I should hardly think his camp experience would induce him to do so. I have had good inducements offered me to enlist, but I made up my mind long ago never to go again, untill I got clear of this enlistment entirely, then if I wish to go again, I can do so at pleasure.

To use your own expression, "I should like to hear from you again if you think you can justify your self in writing to me." You need not be alarmed about my getting tired reading your letters. I send my best regards to all old school-mates. I close hoping this letter will be read in the spirit it is written, in that of kindness.

Yours sincerely,
Will

On the 6th of February the troops were ordered to move out. General Butler had decided that he would take Richmond by a grand cavalry dash, and the Army of the Potomac was to make a demonstration across the Rapidan. Sawyer's group was taken by surprise. They were to take three days rations and move by daylight

The rebels were entrenched and occupied rifle pits down to the river which was swollen and full of ice. They also had artillery in position on the heights which could completely cover the river. The troops were ordered to cross. Some of the shorter men were in water up to their necks but the 8th succeeded in crossing and was able to find cover. Colonel Carroll ordered the men to get into a sunken road and maintain cover for the other troops which were crossing. They were able to maintain well directed fire and soon checked the rebel line, which retreated and took shelter behind fences and buildings which were beyond the fire of the regiment.

Sawyer said, "With the exception of the Eighth Regiment, the division, in the meantime , withdrew to the bank of the river and established in line. We were ordered to fall back to our position in the brigade, but in so doing had to pass over an interval of about five hundred yards in point blank range of the rebel guns and rifles.

"As we emerged from our sunken road the minie balls hissed about us, and occasionally a shell exploded close to us, covering us with mud and dirt.

"The skirmish line during this fight was gallantly commanded by Capt. J. E. Gregg of Co. E, and so skillfully handled that every man was brought off, though it became pitch dark before he could leave the front of the enemy.

"A few casualties occurred. One man received a wound in the abdomen and the writer received a blow from a ball that tore up his haversack, striking the right wrist with a force like that of a sling slung shot, which was very painful, and rendered the hand quite useless for a long time. Several of the men received slight wounds.

"About midnight we re-crossed the river on the bridge that had been built during the day, and in a cold and drenching rain, without fire or shelter, lay down on brush or the bare ground and shivered until morning when fires were built, arms stacked and the troops ordered to remain in their position, making themselves as comfortable as possible.

"After dark the troops returned to camp, General Butler's project having failed. Our division, in furtherance thereof, having cost the two divisions of the Second Corps that crossed the river over two hundred and fifty men in killed and wounded."

Will only briefly mentions this battle and then, with a sense of humor, referring to it only as the indulgence of a cold bath.

Camp 8th OVI
Feb 14th, 1864

Dear Leah,

I must again thank you for being the recipient of a very welcome letter last evening. Let me say one word about my last letter and I will never refer to the subject again while we correspond with each other. As you say it was a strange letter, and one that should never have been written. I had been receiving a great deal of just such news as you speak about and it had been coming so long that I had got tired of it. One correspondent going so far as to tell me just when I was coming to Albion on furlough, and that I was to be married soon after getting there. Now such reports don't concern me in the least but it is different with you. You live among them and can't help but hear it everyday. At least if reports I get is true my letter was written to have a better understanding between us.

I would have given anything to have recalled that letter two days after it was written. It made me look ridiculous in my own eyes, but let us drop the subject for the present. Should I ever have the pleasure of seeing you, I will explain it fully.

You say truly that our correspondence is growing dull. I suppose it is my fault. For the next two months I will try and work a little more spice in my composition. I have done enough corresponding this winter to write a good letter by this time, but every time lately in writing to you nothing but that tarnation gossip gets in my head and spoils it all.

I shall most assuredly call around as you advise and if the collection is interesting enough to make it pay, I will have it published in book form and start out pedling it around the country for a living. Or probably a better plan would be to write for it now while I've got these long winter evenings at my disposal and get it ready, so that I need lose no time when I get out.

I will take your advice, which do you think best. I suppose they think a great deal of me and do of them at any rate, but enough now for camp news.

We have had religious services today at Division Headquarters. The Div was all out and formed a hollow square. We listened to a very eloquent discourse from one of the clergymen attached to the Christian Commission. A great many fair ladies graced the occasion with their presence. We have a chapel erected belonging to our Brigade in which there is services held twice every Sabbath, good or bad weather.

We have also a literary society in the brigade. It meets every Friday evening when we are regaled with a debate or a lecture, and last of all, we have a school. I need not tell you that I belong to it. We have recitation twice a week. My studies are Grammar and Mathematics. I do not make much headway as duty interferes a great deal. You will see that we are not wanting in amusements nor instruction to help pass away the dull hours of camp life.

You have seen by the papers that we have recently been over on a visit to our Rebel friends. I need not tell you that they received us warmly, and treated us to the indulgence of a cold bath, both of which we were not very well pleased with, though I am certain they give us the best they had. Well, this is St. Valentine's Day. Today Cupid flies over the land, in the shape of delicate missives from you and maidens fair. It will soon be the hour for the soldiers mail. Will I get a Valentine? It is possible. Well, the mail has come and no valentines for poor me, nor letters either. Well better luck tomorrow evening. Mine is a valentine for you and I will close.

> *I would not that any form should rise*
> *Before thee in the hours of glee*
> *But when thou thinkest on friends sincere*
> *I wish thee to remember me.*

Yours in friendship,
Will

The troops remained in camp for the rest of the winter and as Sawyer said "no further military operations on the part of the enemy disturbed us until the commencement of the overland campaign."

Will had much time on his hands and so he wrote many letters to his friends in Indiana and Ohio and two of them to Leah written in March. One indicates his concern over the gossip in Albion and the second tells of his study opportunities in camp and mentions his brother Adam (A.J.) and Hannah Haney. Camp 8th 0. V. 1. March 7, 1864

Dear Leah,

Again I have the pleasure of acknowledging the receipt of another of your welcome letters. It found me as usual cogitating over what I'd best do to spend the evening. So you see your letter came just in the right nick of time for there is nothing suits me better than to spend an hour or two in social intercourse with a friend even though the pen is the medium of communication. What does not the world owe to to the person who first discovered the way of putting thoughts upon paper. He certainly was a benefactor of the human race. I have to thank him for many pleasant hours spent during the past winter that would have otherways hung heavy on my hands. But I hope soon to be able to spend many pleasenter hours without having recourse to the pen.

You speak of my letters to the Aid Society and imagine that I know the Alitho..(?) am slightly acquainted with him and I know that he appreciates the Gift and the donors of it still more. I tell you, Leah, and I know what I say there is not words enough in the English language to tell how the soldiers of this army, and of all our armies, appreciate the works of the Aid Societies and the Christian and Sanitary commissions for their efforts in their behalf. how many hundreds of our brave comrades who are now enjoying life and all its pleasures would have this day been under the cold sod, but for the kind offices of some of the members of those associations, but enough.

I don't know but I will take your advice and write for that collection. I can straiten it out before I get home and so have the more time for enjoyment after I get there, by the by. I will give you a little quotation from a letter received in the same mail with yours. "..says Miss Crispell wrote you something about her, and when you get home it is to be fixed up." Now of course you know and so do 1, that it's all humbug. I write two you because it may account for a certain coolness you speak of. This is all confidential between us. I've no business repeating what is sent to me, but have departed from my rule in this case because I thought it would enlighten you to what would otherwise be a mystery. I am expecting to get raked over the coals in all directions when I get back, but if the fire becomes to hot, I can do as the "Army of the Potomac" very often does, that is..retreat.

You ask me for a full description of our reconnaissance across the Rapidan. it occured so long ago that I can hardly recollect the details, but I remember distinctly of wading a cold, deep stream and having innumberable little bullets, big bullets, and all sorts of bullets, whistling in uncomfortable proximity to our heads, though I am happy to say but one of our company was hit, though we must recollect that there is but ten in the company to get hit. Just half the number we lost at Antietam.

I have written full enough for this time. No doubt you find plenty mistakes in my letters as I hardly ever look them over for correction. If I do undertake it I always find so many that I generally throw the whole letter away rather than do that I let the reader correct it. It is selfish I know but then that runs in the family, and I am no better than the rest.

Yours in Friendship.

Will

Camp 8th O.V. I.
March 25th, 1864

Dear Leah,

Again I have the pleasure of replying to a very welcome letter from you. I have just returned from our Lyceum where I had the pleasure of listening to a very interesting lecture by the Chaplain of the 81st Penn. Regt. His subject was "The Characteristics of a True Soldier." He did the subject justice, and that is as much as I need say about it in this. I have never passed a plesenter winter in my life than I have this. Almost every evening there has been someplace of amusement or instruction to attend, and I have had but a small amount of duty to do when compared with the rest. My posision does not bring me on duty as often as what our commissioned officers are and I have enjoyed good health. What cause have I for complaint, none. And taking it all through my term of service, it is the same. It is true at times I have found fault but what even in civil life when enjoying the comforts and blessings of home does not find occasions for complaining. When I compare my case with my comrades, I find cause to be thankful. We have men in our company who have been wounded three times and but very few who have not been in hospital sick, more or less. While I have escaped thus far unscathed. I might fill the sheet with this subject but it is useless.

I am glad to know that you have so good an opinion of Mr. Hardenburg. I had not heard of him for nearly two years. Our Reg fought side by side at Winchester, and one of the hardest fought battles of the war (numbers considered.) The army is a good school but the pupils are not always trained for the best. And now I will speak of a subject that I had hoped never to write of in a letter agin. There was a line in my last letter that ought not to have been in it.

"But, I wrote the foolish fancy of my brain;
The aimless words that, striking, hath caused pain'
The idle words that I've wished back again."

It was no jealous hand that wrote the words I copied in my letter. They were wrote by brother Adam, and by credited to Miss Hannah Haney, though she knew nothing of his writing them to me. Now, Leah, if you will do me a favor you will not say anything about it to her, or any person else. Let them go untill I return when we will straiten matters up. If I never return it's best unsaid. I had thought once of writing to Hannah, but since I have thought it over I have concluded not to.

Let them speak and write what they please. I shall respect you none the less for it. You have never wrote anything to me about any person but what you could say to their faces. As to when I shall get home is a matter of doubt. Our time should be out on the 23rd of April but they may possibly keep us until the 24th of June. We enlisted for three months in the first place and afterwards for three years, with the understanding that our time was to date from first enlistment, but our officers being inexperienced did not make out the rolls in quite the right shape. So they may possible hold us untill the 24th of June. Should we get out in April you will see me about the middle of May if in June and all goes well, I will try and be there on the 4th of July. But let it be when it will. I assure you that you will be one of the first friends I shall call on. Il send you a paper with this. It speaks for itself. I shall expect a few more letters from you ere I see you personly, and in the meantime, remember I am as usual, your friend.

   Will

The next letter written to Leah was during this time period. He is still complaining about the rain and talks about the rebels pickets on the opposite side of the river within speaking distance . He also reminisences about his enlistment since it was three years to the date of the letter he has written.

       Camp 8th O. V. I.
        April 17th 1864

Dear Leah.

 Yours of 2nd inst found me four days ago on the banks of the Rapidan on picket guard. I just got back to camp yesterday evening. We have about five miles to go on picket. We remain three days at a time. We had a rough time of it as it rained almost all the time we were out, but as I have only to go on once a month I can stand it. The rebels picket the opposite bank of the river within easy speaking distance at places. We never fire on another and to do so would be little better than murder in my estimation. Well this is probably the last I will write you from camp for we will move ere many days pass away. Everything appears to in readiness and all that delays it is the bad weather. It rains three days out of a week.

 It is just three years ago this evening since I first signed my name for to go a soldiering. I well recollect the excitement in the north at that time. On that evening there was a meeting called to raise a company of volunteers in the town that I was in (Bucyrus). The hall was crowded. After a number of stirring speeches had been made a call was made for volunteers to come up to the speakers stand put down their names. Well as I recollect the crowd and confusion there then everyone seemed to want to put his name down first. My name was second on the list. That evening one hundred and seven names were signed. A few days after that saw us in Camp Taylor, Cleveland, Ohio serving Uncle Sam.

 I might follow the history of that company up from that day to this, but it would not prove very interesting to you and besides I have already given it to you in my letters from time to time. The time of our discharge is not positively called yet. A great many think we will be discharged on the twenty-fourth of this month, but I don't think it is certain at all for the government needs the services of every man in approaching conflict and they will keep us. I for one shall not complain, as I should like to be at the taking of Richmond. We have been knocking at the gate for nearly three years and I would not like to return at this day without first entering. You must excuse me for not writing a letter of more interest. I am not very bright this evening but as I shall have but few more letters to write. Once I can see you personly it does not matter so much for I am a great deal better talker than I am a writer and I will be able to speak of things that can not be put in paper. Hoping to hear from you again, I will close with my best wishes for your happiness.

Yours truly,
Will

General Grant had taken over the command of the army and preparations for its thorough reorganization were everywhere. The Second Corps was completely remodeled and was organized in four divisions. General Hancock had recovered from his wounds and resumed command. The Second Division, 3rd Brigade was headed by Col. S. S. Carroll. On the 22nd of April, General Grant reviewed the Corps and most of the officers and men saw him for the first time. They were greatly impressed and all looked forward to the most complete victory under "Old Unconditional Surrender," as the men called the Commander-in-chief.

On the 3rd of May 1864, the grand army drew out of its winter camp and the campaign of the "Wilderness" was commenced.

The morning report of the 8th Regiment showed present for duty 18 officers and two hundred and thirty-five enlisted men. There were twelve commissioned officers absent on detached service, and on sick leave, and of enlisted men there were absent, sick and on furlough, forty.

On quitting camp that day the army advanced rapidly toward the Rapidan in two columns. The Second Corps was the left of the column. A cavalry division had laid down a canvas pontoon bridge which the Second Corps rapidly crossed on its way to Chancellorsville, and arrived on the old battle ground early on the morning of the 4th of May. They remained there on the same field where they had fought under General Hooker the year before.

The next day, the 5th of May, a heavy column under command of Sedgwick and Warren crossed on the right and now confronted Lee with over one hundred thousand men. All knew that a great battle was soon to be fought. The eighth had been on the same ground twice before; at Chancellorsville and Mine Run, the memory of which was not a happy one, but now the men felt anxious for the battle and confident of their victory.

It was a hot morning and the march was difficult through the brush and cedar. The men suffered from lack of water and the heat. The roar of guns could be heard in the distance. The troops passed over the Brock Road in the afternoon and came upon the battle field. Trees were scarred and splintered and a good many dead and wounded lay in the path. The Second Division of the Sixth Corps under General Getty, had been engaged here in a desperate battle with the rebels under Hill. A few hundred yards away were a couple of big guns which had been lost by Getty and which were now turned on the Second Corps. Colonel Carroll ordered the 8th Ohio to retake the guns; which was done. The 7th Virginia moved up on the north side of the road and the Eighth Ohio on the south side. The skirmishers were in front until the captured guns had been passed about 100 yards. Then a few men with drag ropes sprung into the road and dragged back the guns. Several men of the Eighth and Seventh were wounded. One Lieutenant very severely, and one man killed. "But we were so much protected by the woods and the movement was so quick, that we had the guns and were back out of reach, before the rebel supports at the guns could be reinforced and they were taken prisoners," Sawyer reported.

By the time Col. Carroll's Brigade had come up to the position the battle had been raging for nearly four hours. In a savage encounter with the rebels General Alexander Hayes, who had recently commanded the division, was killed. When it became dark the battle stopped as both sides lay on their arms to wait for the next day's battle.

During the night supplies were replenished and the men slept fitfully beside their weapons. At four o'clock the men were aroused and ordered to have a cold breakfast and be ready to move at five A.M.

Sawyer commented," In a few minutes, we heard the opening shots from our front, which were promptly replied to by the enemy. We moved on rapidly over the ground fought over yesterday; the trees being cut and splintered in some instances so as to look like hickory brooms. We soon passed the line where the rebels had rested during the night, as was evident from the corn meal, Johnny cake, etc, strewn about on the ground. We were now driving the enemy rapidly, keeping up a running fire, and cheering lustily as we supposed we were having the battle all our own way. About a mile and half from camp, the presence of a heavy force became apparent.

"We were on the south side of the road and Col. Carroll ordered the 14th Indiana and the 8th Ohio across the road with Col. Coons of the Fourteenth Indiana in command. We commenced to move by the right flank with the fourteenth Indiana in front. That regiment had barely cleared the road, when it was furiously attacked. Col. Coons faced to the front and opened fire, ordering the Eighth to move past his regiment, file into line, and commence firing as soon as possible. This we did as best we could. The fire now was severe, and as we moved forward to a considerable ridge, we almost fell into the embrace of the whole of Longstreet's Corps. The woods were literally black with ranks of men as far as we could see. A terrific volley of fire struck us and our officers and men went down all along the line.

"Col. Coons and I were on horseback and we could see that we had to get out of that. We sent the colors back and moved the men as carefully as we could. One Captain was killed, one had been severely wounded and 18 men were killed and wounded and two so badly wounded that they could not be rescued. Two men were taken prisoners and carried to Andersonville.

"The balance of the Brigade, on the south side of the plank road had already fallen back, and the Eighth Ohio and Fourteenth Indiana were now quite alone; still the retreat was made in good order. We received orders to fall back to our previous night's position.

"The Eighth was ordered to support a detachment of artillery and cavalry as it guarded the left flank which General Hancock feared would be attacked. After moving up on the road about two miles, we opened out into the woods; the cavalry dashed forward but no enemy appeared. The commander being satisfied that there was no enemy in front, we fell back to our brigade at the junction of the Brock and Plank roads.

"In the meantime strong earth and log works, with an abattis* (* A network of felled trees in front of an entrenched position, with branches interlaced and facing the enemy's position to form an obstacle to attacking troops. From the Encyclopedia of the Civil War.) in front had been thrown up along the west side of the Brock Road, which were now heavily manned, and awaiting the onset of the enemy. The Regiment was not united with the Brigade which was in the second line.

"About five o'clock in the afternoon the rebels began to shell us preparatory to a general charge on our works. Presently their column came on, cheering and yelling like yahoos. It was the famous rebel yell. Our line was formed, ready to support the men in the breastworks, and a battery at the cross roads sent its heavy missiles crashing through the woods towards the enemy.

Far along to our right was the rattle of musketry and the roar of artillery, telling of the general battle all along the line. Warren's, Burnside's and Sedgwick's as well as our Second corps, in close grapple with the enemy.

"On came the columns of Longstreet, dashing furiously into the abattis, when our artillery and musketry opened upon them like a tornado. Forward swept our line, and as the boys saw the struggling rebels in the bush, the woods and the abattis, and some few inside of our works, they could hardly be kept in line. Carroll's whole brigade, cheering louder and louder, rushed forward, and joining with the front line, fell upon the charging columns routing them in every direction.

"The rebel loss was terrible, and their broken columns fell back not again to renew the contest at this point. The battle along the whole line had been most obstinately fought on both sides. In fact one of the most terrible battles of the war had been fought.

Colonel Sawyer quotes from the Campaigns of the Army of the Potomac by Swinton "a battle terrible and indescribable in these gloomy woods. There is something horrible, yet fascinating, in the mystery shrouding this strangest of battles ever fought , a battle which no man could see, and whose progress could only be followed by the ear, as the sharp and crackling volleys of musketry and the alternate Union cheer and Confederate yell told how the fight surged and swelled. The battle continued two days; yet such was the mettle of each combatant that it decided nothing. It was in every respect a demon battle; and its only result appeared in the tens of thousands of dead and wounded in blue and gray that lay in the thick woods. The Union loss exceeded fifteen thousand, and the confederate loss was about eight thousand."

This is the spot where Alexander Spotswood dug the first iron ore and built the first iron furnace on the continent, about 1720 at Germania Ford. The name of the county, Spottsylvania, is derived from his name by latinizing the last syllable.

The battles continued over this area for several days with the Eighth losing many of its men including Col. Sawyer who was severely wounded and was removed to Fredericksburg, Maryland. This was the largest hospital area and probably among the best. Senator John Sherman of Ohio and others of note visited the wounded and tried to soothe them. Sawyer was transported to the hospital in Washington, D. C.

After this the Eighth was ordered to the front, this time being North Anna. They were met by Lee and severe fighting resulted. The Eighth Regiment lost five men killed and seven wounded. Grant shifted his battle line several times . The fight continued through May 28th when the Brigade reached the Pamunkey River. The Eighth was at the head of most of the skir-

mishes. On June first, they again skirmished with Lee's troops losing ten men. Again, they were put on night march to Cold Harbor. June 3rd the Brigade was engaged in severe fighting. The rebels broke the Union ranks and the men could not advance. In this battle the Union army lost over thirteen thousand men. At this point the Fourth Ohio and the Fourteenth Indiana was relieved from battle. Its term of service was over leaving only the Eighth Ohio on the battle line.

The next communication from W. F. Kimmell was written to Leah with barely a word about the severe battles his Eighth Ohio Volunteer Infantry had been in.

In the Pine Woods near Richmond
June 7th, 1864

Dear Leah,

I received your letter some time ago. Opportunities for writing have been scarce. I had made up my mind at one time not to attempt to write at all but as half a chance has occured, I will drop you a line. I've no pen nor ink with me so I have to pencil it. We have been having a hard campaign of it—since the 8th of May but thanks to Providence and our doughty little Lieut-Gen we have been so far successful and with every prospect of continuing so. We are now within eight miles of Richmond. I am writing this about three hundred yards from the rebel works. They are laying very quiet just now. About sundown we will have a little excitement. That is the time that we generaly advance our skirmish line and we always have a little fight over it. I don't think we will have any more as hard fighting to do as we have had. It will be done with the pick and shovel. I have just been out in the trenches. We can count six rebel flags from there. If we get along as fast in the next two days as we have in the past they will move them. I will bring this to a close. I don't think you'd better answer this as we hardly remain in the field long enough to get it. We expect to be in Columbus Ohio by the 24th of the month. If so, I will be at home on the 4th of July. Hoping that I may weather the storm until then and see you personaly. I close my last soldier letter to you.

Yours truly
W. F. Kimmell

Colonel Sawyer closes his narrative by stating that after the 5th of June when the Fourth Ohio left for home , only the 8th Ohio and the 7th West Virginia of the Brigade were on the battle field. "On the night of the 12th of June, the Second Corps fell back, and marching all night, reached the Chickahominy River about noon on the 13th, and crossing the river reached Charles City Court House after dark. The Eighth had passed through this place on the 17th of August 1862, after the evacuation of Harrison's Landing, and the men were disposed to recount their many adventures since. The Second Corps reached James River in the evening, at a place called Windmill Point. Here the river was crossed, and the the 15th marched to the line at Petersburg. Another fierce battle ensued with the regiment being under fire most of the time until June 24 when the order came relieving the Regiment from duty, and ordering it home to be mustered out, its full term of three years service having been fulfilled.

"At the command, About Face, the officers and men gathered up their traps, and bade farewell to their friends, the booming cannon, the 'Johnies' and started for City Point with light hearts and elastic steps.

"At City Point , the Regiment embarked on the "Highland Light" and steamed away for Washington, where it arrived next day at noon. After considerable delay in getting rations and transportation for the journey, the train drew out of the depot at ten o'clock at night. We were ordered to Columbus, Ohio. The men were very jolly and but little sleep was indulged in. When breakfast time came it was discovered that no rations had been put aboard. With some harsh words from the men, they all got food from their haversacks and took care of their needs.

"We reached the Ohio River a little after noon, and re-crossed at the same point where we had crossed into Dixie on the 9th day of July, 1861. The sight of the grand old river—no longer a dividing line between slavery and freedom—was the signal for many a cheer and many quaint apostrophes. Some sang and some cried—we were again in Ohio—we were home.

"We arrived at Columbus about 10 o'clock in the evening, only to be ordered to Cleveland. This involved a change of cars and another all night ride. However, rations were procured and towards midnight we got started for Cleveland, where we arrived Sunday morning, July 3rd, 1864.

"We were met at the cars by Mayor Senter and a delegation of the Military Committee and citizens headed by the Temperance Brass Band and escorted to Wheeler and Russell's dining Hall, where an excellent breakfast had been prepared by order of the Military Committee of Cleveland.

"After doing the most ample justice to the breakfast, the mayor welcomed the regiment in a most happy speech in which he recounted the deeds of bravery, patriotism and self-sacrifice in our country's service, mentioning the men who had fallen in service. After many responses and cheers, a procession was formed, the city police in full uniform leading the way, followed by the brass band, and other officals with the regiment bearing its tattered colors and disabled soldiers in carriages. We moved through the streets directly to Camp Cleveland where the soldiers were comfortably lodged.

"On Monday, the 4th of July was celebrated in true old fashioned patriotic style, with speeches and band numbers. The regiments (7th, 8th and 24th) returned to their quarters. The muster rolls and balance sheets were prepared as rapidly as possible by the commandants of companies and finally on the 13th day of July, 1864, the Eighth Regiment, Ohio Volunteers was duly mustered out of service. The number present for muster was one hundred and sixty-eight. The number of absent—prisoners, wounded and sick, who also were mustered out—was over two hundred, besides those serving in the 4th Ohio Battalion."

The roster of company C shows that William F. Kimmell, Sgt., was wounded at Winchester and Spotsylvania and discharged July 13, 1864 missing his goal of being at home on the 4th of July by nine days.

SUGGESTED REFERENCES

Kennedy, Francis H., ed. **The Civil War Battlefield Guide**. The Conservation Fund. Houghton Mifflin, Co., 1990.

Wheeler, Richard. **Witness To Gettysburg.** Harper & Row. 1987.

Editors of theAmerican Heritage - The Magazine of History. **Picture History of the Civil War.** American Heritage Publ. Co. Bonanza Books, New York.

James E. McPherson and Richard Gottlieb, Editors. **Battle Chronicles of the Civil War 1862.** MacMillan Publishing Co.

Harper's History of the Great Rebellion., The Fairfax Press

War Department. **The War of the Rebellion, A compilation of the Official records of the Union and Confederate Armies**. Series I Volume XIX, Vol XXI. U. S. Government Printing Office. 1887.

Wiley,Bell Irvin. **The Life of Billy Yank**. Louisiana State University Press. 1981 reprint.

Wiley, Bell Irvin. **The Life of Johnny Reb**. Louisiana State University Press. 1982 reprint.

W.F. INDEX

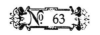

CPSIA information can be obtained at www.ICGtesting.com
Printed in the USA
BVOW040716210312

285661BV00003B/1/P